P9-CAS-689

connecting
art to stitch

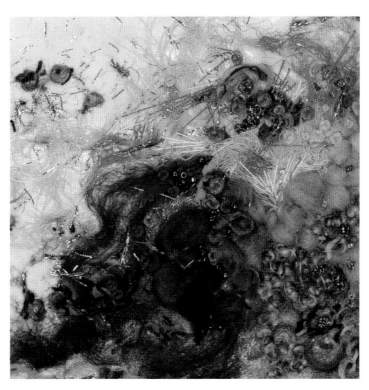

connecting
art to stitch

Sandra Meech

BATSFORD

Acknowledgements

My thanks go to textile friends and colleagues who have
contributed their art to this book, and to Michael Wicks for
his wonderful photography. The continued support and
encouragement from Jan Beaney, Jean Littlejohn, Sybil
Rampen, the members of 'Quilt Art', and many students
everywhere has meant a great deal to me. However, special
thanks go to my family for their uncompromising patience
and consideration over the years.

First published in the United Kingdom in 2009 by
Batsford
10 Southcombe Street
London
W14 0RA

An imprint of Anova Books Company Ltd

Copyright © Batsford 2009
Text and illustrations © Sandra Meech 2009

The moral rights of the author have been asserted.

All rights reserved. No part of this publication may be
reproduced, stored in a retrieval system, or transmitted in
any form or by any means, mechanical, photocopying,
recording or otherwise, without the prior permission of the
copyright owner.

ISBN 978 1 9063 8810 2

A CIP catalogue record for this book is available from the
British Library.

17 16 15 14 13 12 11 10 09
10 9 8 7 6 5 4 3 2 1

Reproduction by Craft Print Ltd, Singapore
Printed and bound by Rival Colour Ltd, UK

This book can be ordered direct from the publisher at the
website www.anovabooks.com, or try your local bookshop.

Distributed in the United States and Canada by
Sterling Publishing Co., 387 Park Avenue South,
New York, NY 10016, USA

Left: **Reykjavik Harbour** (Sandra Meech, UK).

Opposite: **Sheer Sketchbook** (Sandra Meech, UK).

CONTENTS

USING THIS BOOK
Getting started 08
Review stitch and surface-design skills 09
Get inspired and organized 11

1 SUBJECTS AND DESIGN 18
Landscape 20
Detail in nature 22
Cityscape – the urban scene 24
Buildings – and architectural detail 25
Still life 26
Drawing from life 29
Collectibles and hobbies 31
Social comment 33
Taking a step into the abstract 34

2 DRAW, SKETCH AND STITCH 36
Materials 38
Using line and tone 41
Charcoal, conté sticks and pencils 44
Pens and markers 46
Coloured pencils 54
Oil and chalk pastels, sticks and pencils 57

3 COLOUR 62
Basic colour exercises 65

4 PAINTING 68
Additional general art materials 71
Watercolour 72
Disperse transfer dyes 76
Gouache 82
Brusho 85
Creating a sketchbook 87
Acrylics 92
Oil paints 101

5 MIXED MEDIA 106
Collage 108
Photo image transfer 111
Mixed-media and print techniques 120
Presenting art textiles 124

CONCLUSION 125
GLOSSARY 126
BIBLIOGRAPHY AND SUPPLIERS 127
INDEX 128

USING THIS BOOK

Making the connection from art to stitch is an essential step for anyone who is passionate about contemporary textiles.

We can easily be seduced by the prospect of yet more stitch techniques and textile products to try, while neglecting to take the time to explore or revisit fine art skills. We may be quite competent quilters or embroiderers, but have little confidence when asked to draw. Or perhaps it is now time to revisit 'art' skills after a long absence. There is a perception that certain people are born with artistic talent, and this may be true to some extent, but with regular practice, creating 'art' can become second nature and begin to impact on the visual strength of new work in stitched textiles.

The habit of seeing the world around us with art and stitch in mind reinforces this important connection – sketched lines become thread 'marks', watercolour washes are sheers, acrylic paint is transformed into shape, pattern or applied fabric. Reviewing design and colour, composition and perspective from the world of fine art will continue to reinforce that link.

A variety of 'fine art' subjects will be considered here: landscape, still life, detail and texture in nature and architecture, drawing from life and the media. You might also choose to develop a personal theme at the same time. Subjects can have a realistic or, for a more contemporary and expressive feel, an abstract approach. Other ideas could be concept-driven, with subtle or explosive colour capturing the essence of the theme. Pattern, texture and shape can also be a dominant starting point for art and can be used to create a change in style that could inform a new stitched-textile art piece. This book will provide a source of basic fine art skills, as materials for drawing, sketching and painting, as well as collage and mixed media, are explored. Exercises in art and stitch and a selection of 'art classes' in each section will offer new creative possibilities. Potential subjects will be suggested, but there are no 'rules' or 'time limits' – it is up to you to explore at your own pace. At all times, the connection with fabric and stitch will be considered, many of the exercises being interchangeable in theme as well as in fabric and sewing options.

Photography is an essential tool for today's textile artist, being used to record, enhance and focus our ideas, while consolidating good composition and design. Digital image software also plays an important role and there are frequent references to filters and photo effects.

Working in sketchbooks and mixed-media collage is also an essential part of the creative process in both art and stitch. Drawings and paintings become the starting point for a new stitch piece. Decisions on appropriate sewing techniques and materials also need to be considered, as well as suggestions as to how textile art should be displayed.

The many wonderful books available on art and stitch are a valuable resource, but they can never go far enough – the personal connection we make between art and stitch every day is the most valuable lesson we can learn.

Right, top to bottom: **Sweet Indulgence** (Freda Surgenor, Australia); **Birthday Cheer** (Sandra Meech, UK); **The Other Side of the Lake #2 (detail)** (Dorothy Caldwell, Canada); **The Bruce Trail** (Sandra Meech, UK).

Left: **Glacier Ice** (Sandra Meech, UK). Print from dilute acrylic on clingfilm.

Getting started

Finding and nurturing the art within you is the first step. You may think, or have been told, that you have no ability, but with practice anything is possible. Give yourself permission to try. No one is watching or making critical comments about your efforts. Just enjoy the experience. You will discover not only new materials, but new art skills that will take your contemporary quilts and stitched textiles to a fresh level.

Creating the space

A comfortable, well-lit (and well-ventilated) environment is necessary. Ideally, this should be a separate room or area where you can store both art materials and sewing needs. Creative ideas, in both art and stitch disciplines, merge together when materials are close at hand.

- Good lighting is essential; natural light is the best, but don't work in your own shadow – an anglepoise lamp with a natural bulb is useful for better colour decisions.
- A planning wall is an important place to pin up ideas, references, sources of inspiration, photographs or your work as it is developing. It's a good practice to stand back and take photographs at different stages, so you can live with your art before making further decisions.
- You will need a general work/sewing table with a slightly raised drawing board for smaller pieces of artwork.
- A table or standing easel would be good for painting on canvas with oils or acrylic; this facilitates broad movements with your brushstrokes.
- A flat table (at kitchen counter height) is best for cutting, ironing and preparing fabric, for printing techniques, such as screen printing or monoprinting, or to provide a raised platform for photographing still-life subjects.
- If space allows, it's good to have a separate work surface for a sewing machine and sundries such as threads and fabrics, allowing easy movement from art to stitch.
- It's useful to have a computer or laptop and printer nearby.
- A bookshelf is essential for your personal library of photo files and notes, as well as for art and stitch books, for reference and inspiration.

Above: **Thistle sketch** (Sandra Meech, UK).
Pen and ink. Below: A studio/workroom space.

Review stitch and surface-design skills

Every time you take a photograph or explore a drawing and painting exercise, however complicated or challenging, always think about the different surface, sewing and stitch techniques that could be combined to achieve a similar result. Art and stitch go hand in hand and the task of creating that final textile piece will be so much easier when consideration has been given to the choice of techniques on offer right from the start. Whatever textile discipline you practise – quiltmaking or embroidery – make a list of all the skills and techniques that you already know. Below is a sample list to start you off, but remember there may be more skills to add to the list.

Piecing methods Two fabrics joined together by hand or machine – simple piecing, curved piecing, paper piecing – all traditional patchwork-style piecing skills.

Appliqué The technique of applying one fabric onto another by hand and machine – with satin-stitch, turned-under, raw-edge or reverse appliqué (look at world textiles for additional methods).

Stitch For the quilter, the **darning stitch** holds fabric layers together and can be made by machine or hand; bigger stitches can be decorative, repetitive, creative, bold, dynamic or delicate marks, used to create movement or enhance colour. Create a list of quilting 'stitch marks' with which you are familiar, such as kantha stitch, tying, knotting, big darning stitches, cross stitches or seeding stitches.

Embroidery stitches come in all shapes and sizes and can be made with thick or thin stranded cottons and wools, built up to create texture and dimension. You can couch any type of material – natural or manmade – onto the surface to create added dimension. French knots (for texture) and big darning stitches (for movement) could go on your list.

Machine stitch on soluble materials (cold- and hot-water opaque material) can form a background for added stitches. Even the build-up of heavily machined thread stitch can cause distortion.

Textural surfaces Consider pleating, folding or ruching of fabric, or dimensional applications with Wireform or the use of shrinkage for distortion, PVA- or gesso-stiffened fabric, butter muslin or scrim stiffened with glue and paint, and needle-felting in layers. Traditional quilt techniques, such as trapunto-stuffed appliqué or yo-yo, could be considered for dimension. In embroidery, pulled thread work and many other styles could be considered for added texture.

Transparency with sheers, including the trapping and bonding of scraps of material, as well as screen printing or painting on transparent fabrics or the use of Perspex and plastics.

Cutting back or cutting through to reveal negative spaces, with light and shadow as part of the design – chenille methods of layering; cutting through for raw-edge colour, and using a heat tool on cotton organzas or non-woven materials such as Lutradur.

Painting and dyeing on cotton or silk or using discharge pastes to take colour away – these effects can be easily achieved. Sometimes trial-and-error approaches to surface fabric design can work well, but any skill will be more satisfying when a degree of direction and control have been acquired, much of which will come through art practice.

Right: A variety of appliqué, embroidery and surface techniques from Sandra Meech, Bailey Curtis (second image down) and Mandy Ginsberg (fifth image down).

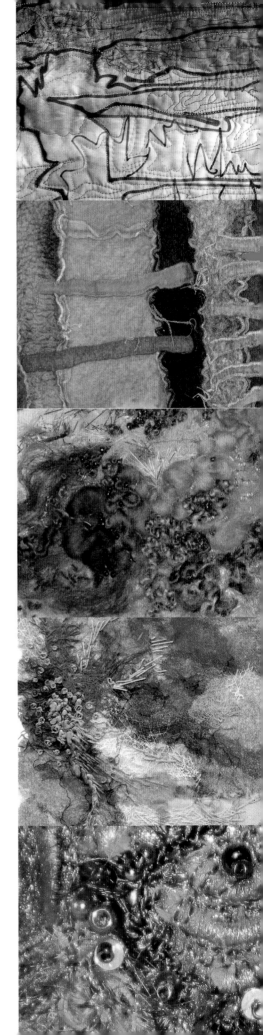

Above: **Stills from A Life** (Dominie Nash, USA).

Fabric surface techniques are also good to add to the list. You will be surprised how many different skills you have learned over time. Wonderful results can be achieved by using simple tie-dye, batik and hand-dyeing methods to create fabrics that look 'abstract' and can be easily incorporated into contemporary art textiles.

Explorations with other surface-design techniques should also be added to the list, including fabric-printing methods, such as stamps, screen printing, monoprinting, collagraphs and lino cuts.

Mixed media and collage Stitching through paper, plastics, leather, wire, string or furnishing fabrics, using lace and net; other dimensional embellishment with beads, sequins or buttons could also be included, so keep these potential mixes of materials in mind.

Photo image transfer methods have become popular – heat transfer papers, used with an inkjet printer or laserjet photocopies and an acrylic medium, can achieve wonderful results on cotton. Photographs or imagery from art could be scanned and included in that final stitched textile.

Lastly, add any art and design knowledge learned over the years. It will be surprising what knowledge of colour theory and principles and elements of design or composition you have acquired at one time or another.

You may be surprised to discover how long your personal list of techniques might be!

Get inspired and organized

It can be very liberating to allow yourself time to enjoy learning about new materials and art techniques through a variety of subjects without the constraints of a finished quilt or embroidery. If you give yourself the freedom to just sketch, try watercolour washes, paint with abandon or create a self portrait in collage you will discover how rewarding this can be. In fact, the experience you acquire through this 'artistic journey' will change your whole approach to your own textiles. Every inspirational photograph, sketched line or painted brushstroke could be interpreted in stitch.

Working from life or using photographs as reference

Both art and stitch practice require a good understanding of line and form, with colour and composition as essential ingredients. Since colour, composition and light are such strong components of drawing and painting, it's best, when possible, to work from real life with a subject that is directly before you. However, the camera can be an extremely useful artistic tool with which to capture that fleeting moment or a change of light. Consider using both ways of working.

Right, top: **Under the Arches** (detail) (Sandra Meech, UK). Bottom: photographs and details from nature, still life and architecture.

11

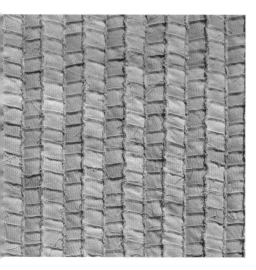

- **For still life**, working directly with the subject gives a fresh approach, but photography can be of value for recording different angles, highlights, cast shadows and textures.
- **A landscape** can change with the time of day or season or according to the weather, and painting or sketching outdoors can bring vitality and energy to a piece. Consider Monet's landscapes – the lightness and vigour of his brushstrokes bear testimony to the value of working in this way. Static textural subjects, such as bark, wood, shells or rock, will always inspire an interesting drawing without the need for a photograph. In nature, however, a detail of a leaf or a flower can often only be achieved with a quick sketch before the subject begins to wilt or curl (effects that can also provide interesting drawings). In such cases, a photograph will record the detail while it is still fresh.

Above and left: **High Tide, Low Tide, Broadstairs** (Inge Hueber, Germany).
Inspiration from the subtle hues of sea and shore. Dyed cotton, with visible seams.

- **Mixed media and collage** often includes photography (your own or copyright-free), printed images, writings, sketches, textured papers, found objects and so on.
- **Portrait or figure drawings** are best drawn from life, but this may not always be possible. On holiday, it may be difficult to sketch people, market scenes or colourful textiles, in which case photography may be the only way to capture the subject.
- **Building and reflections** change quickly as the light alters and photographs offer a useful means of recording detail and perspective.
- **Abstract art** may be inspired by photos, but becomes an expressive 'impression' of the original subject. Enlarged details from photographs can also inspire art.

Above: **Pentimento #28** (Jette Clover, Belgium). Mixed fabrics, printed imagery and stitch.

Photography for reference

In the last ten years the camera, the computer and the printer have become additional tools for the textile artist. Digital cameras make the recording of imagery and detail so easy. Software packages, such as Photoshop Elements or Paint Shop Pro, have made it fun. As an extension to our repertoire, even computer-programmed sewing machines can draw with machine stitches. It is essential for all stitched-textile artists to know how to provide good high-resolution images on a disc for open competitions or exhibition opportunities, so taking good photos of our work is a major consideration.

All digital cameras are different, but it is worth considering the following:
- Get a camera with at least 6 million + megapixels for a good 12½ x 17½cm (5 x 7in) image, a telephoto/zoom facility and a macro or close-up mode.
- The software program that comes with a digital camera is often user-friendly, but programs such as Picasa (from Google) can be downloaded free off the internet; Photoshop Elements or Paint Shop Pro are affordable and have an interesting assortment of filters and artistic effects that can be explored for creative photography.
- As a record of our work, digital images are immensely valuable – they can be sent over the internet as a jpg – files usually no larger than 2 or 3 MB, or smaller resolutions for sharing. A knowledge of digital imagery is useful for personal website planning and the increased use of blog sites makes an immediate picture or illustration accessible to all.
- Printing photographs directly from the computer at home can offer great flexibility in our busy lives.

Left, top to bottom: **Peter and Jared**; **Beach Huts at Lyme**; **Torn Posters**; **Waterlogged** (all Sandra Meech, UK).

Above: **Shimmering Rocks** (Sandra Meech, UK).

Photography as art

For years, the role of photography in observing nature or documenting society has been considered an art form, although it is not always accepted as seriously as it should be in the 'art world'. The camera has become a valuable tool of the fine artist – a constant reminder of good composition, as we record landscapes, detail in nature and everyday life around us.

A black-and-white image will help with tonal values; quick tracings of detail could inspire line that will become 'stitch'. Digital images can be viewed on a computer screen, resized or cropped, for a more abstract approach, or an enlarged image can be projected onto a wall to provide a starting point for a large drawing or textile piece. This is not cheating: the tools of the 21st century are available to us for use, just as the camera obscura revolutionized the process of enlarging an image centuries ago. Today, fine-art installations often include video imagery in dynamic and exciting ways.

Above: **Imagine** (Lura Schwartz Smith, USA).

Right: **Jared** (Sandra Meech, UK)

Quick coloured-pencil sketch.

Left: acrylic, gouache and silk paints.
Right: Various reference photographs. Clockwise from top left: coloured pencils; a contemplative ewe; Vancouver crabs; pond algae; an iceberg lagoon; leaf droplets (all Sandra Meech, UK).
Below left: Rusted, textured corrugated walls.

Gathering materials together

Art materials can seem vast in range and scope, daunting and expensive, but student-quality art materials are quite adequate to begin with. First see what you already have – you may be surprised how much you have already accumulated. A good variety of drawing and mark-making equipment is essential, as the regular practice of sketching and drawing is fundamental to all media and stitch. If you work in black and white initially, you will be able to consider line, shape and tone without having to make colour choices. The basic materials needed are listed in a chart on page 70.

Photographs Prints or digital images (in files on the computer) should be organized into different subject categories so references are easy to find. You might start with subjects such as landscapes, architecture, natural textures (rock, pebbles, shells and so on), industrial imagery, people, still life, flowers, reflections, and clouds and sky.

Research on a new subject could come from books or the internet; mixed with your own experiences and feelings this could provide a 'written' element to your work. It's also a good habit to keep a file of newspaper and magazine articles.

Above and left (detail): **Winter Wheat**
(Elizabeth Brimelow, UK).

SUBJECTS AND DESIGN

1

Before now, your inspiration may have come from a design in a book, a project in a 'techniques' workshop or colourful experiments with surface design and art cloth. These approaches certainly have their merit, but ultimately you are not the one in control of how the final stitched textile will look.

A more rewarding way is to create ideas and images on paper (or canvas) first, then decide how they could be achieved in stitch. Hopefully, practising drawing and sketching, as well as revisiting colour, design and composition, will become second nature, as these habits are essential to a richer approach to stitch. Giving yourself permission to explore, record and collect information, make diary observations and take photographs will make every creative journey more satisfying.

This chapter focuses on a variety of subjects, with important design and composition considerations to stimulate new ideas, perhaps on a personal theme.

There is no better place to see the best examples of fine art techniques, composition, use of colour and subjects than in a contemporary art gallery. From realism to abstract works, we can learn so much by just looking at how artists have expressed and interpreted their chosen subjects with sensitivity, boldness, colour and drama. This can't help but influence our own future work.

Above: **Shingle** (Elizabeth Brimelow, UK).

Landscape

Most stitched-textile artists have at one time been inspired by landscape. Much of 'who we are' comes from where we live and it continues to be evident everywhere how much landscape influences us. Subjects may be close to home, such as ploughed fields or the back garden, or you might be inspired by a holiday view, such as the beach, olive groves, mountains or deserts. Whatever the case, we find this 'sense of place' one of the most alluring subjects to draw, paint or stitch.

A panorama, whether viewed for sketching, painting or photography, helps us see colour, composition and perspective through changing light, shadows, distant horizons, winding paths and foreground detail. A stitched-textile piece can go further, as our own memories, experiences or historical knowledge can become evident.

▶ *Gather landscape photographs from your last holiday. Does a pattern emerge with the type of landscapes you like? Record the exact location, time of day and any memories. Subjects close to home often supply the richest sources of inspiration and memories, yet we often forget to 'see' what is on our doorstep.*

The rule of thirds Based on the golden-section rectangle, this important rule of proportion remains instrumental in contemporary design composition and is also used in art and photography. A centre of interest, or focal point, is one of the junction points at which an area is broken into thirds, vertically and horizontally. The chosen centre of interest is balanced with another point of interest in the opposite corner. The viewer's eye then moves around the composition to best advantage (see A, left).

Left: Dynamic focal point examples taken from an original view at Lyme Regis.

Left: **Down the Lane**
(Bailey Curtis, UK). Right:
Collage of painted and
textured papers used as
inspiration. Right and below:
Use aperture Ls to find an
interesting, abstract area;
study perspective from a
favourite photo.

'Window' templates An 'L'-shaped aperture or rectangular window (perhaps the same proportion as a favourite sketchbook) is a useful tool for any sketching or observation of detail. Consider how artists use the natural 'L' shape made by their thumb and index finger to isolate information in a landscape.

Perspective Perspective is used in art to form the illusion of three dimensions – distant features near the horizon line look small; middle-distance subjects larger, and detail in the foreground the biggest. This can create great depth. One-point perspective is the easiest to illustrate and perhaps the most commonly used in painting, often with the point being outside the image. Abstract approaches to perspective could show no visible vanishing point where detail is flat.

Sketchbooks Sketchbooks adapt perfectly to landscape subjects. Landscape-shaped bound or spiral sketchbooks are the most practical. See page 87 for more sketchbook possibilities in pencil, pen, coloured pencils and watercolour. Easy to transport, sketchbooks are great for all subjects and an ideal place in which to record drawings, paintings, ideas and personal writings and to experiment with a mix of media.

Right: **Sand Dunes in the Outback** (Sandra Meech, UK).
Landscape inspiration.

Detail in nature

Natural subjects – for example shells, stones, bark, seed pods, flowers, leaves – are perfect still-life subjects for drawing and painting. Many natural subjects can become dynamic designs for art quilts and embroidery. Historical garments, decoration and woven tapestries often depict vines, leaves, birds and flowers, all rich in colour and stitch.

From collected photos you can amass an endless list of potential subjects – water reflections, waves on the sea, seaweed, pebbles on the beach, lichen or images of birds, butterflies or animals. Sketching outdoors will capture the true essence of the subject, but backup digital images are a good reference.

We can use detail in nature to learn to observe both texture and colour closely, using composition and lighting to highlight the negative shapes before us, while practising drawing and sensitivity of line and shape. Make a habit of observing flowers and plants through the seasons as they come into bud or change colour. Gather bits of bark, rock, shells and seed pods (garden centres are a great source in any season) for colour, texture and pattern as subject matter.

Tone and tonal sketching values Tone has a variety of meanings in art. It may refer to the use of light and shade to define a subject and can also be used to relate to colour – the tints and shades of a hue or colour. Conveying tonal values in black and white can easily be practised with soft pencil or charcoal, using the classic rectangle, cone and circular shape. A simple subject, such as a white jug or cup, is straightforward; even an orange, pear, shell or seed pod could be used, if placed with a strong light source on one side.

Scaling up a drawing The practice of enlarging a small reference image to fill a larger area has been used by artists through the ages. Use a window template or L-shaped pieces of card to select an area, then scale it up to translate the image from one place to another.

Break the subject area into equal portions and, using a piece of acetate or tracing paper, draw a small grid on the chosen area, and larger squares in the same proportion in your sketchbook. Look from square to square to copy the outline of the basic shapes. Once this is done, it will be easy to add colour and detail.

Top: Images from nature.
Above: **White Jug**. Pencil sketch to show examples of light and shade.

Right: Walls of China, Lake Mungo, Australia.

Above and right: Squares are drawn on a layer of acetate, and larger squares are drawn in pencil onto painted sketchbook pages, ready for transferring the image.

Sketchbook approaches Full sketchbook pages of scaled drawings and detail in any medium can be an inspiration. Use a double-page spread to include several details of a subject at different angles and sizes, filling the whole spread, with some images bleeding off the pages. Remember that a pale wash of colour on the sketchbook page will be less daunting than blank white.

Above: The sketchbook spread is completed with coloured pencil.
Below: **Mungo Sunrise** (Sandra Meech, UK). More sketchbook inspiration from Australia.

Cityscape – the urban scene

Photographs can provide snapshots of everyday life, showing the hustle and bustle of people going about their daily lives. Travel images can capture very different scenes: urban dwellings and hill towns in bright colours, so different from our own, boats in marinas, alleyways or private walled gardens. Close-up details – cobblestones, wall textures, peeling paint, wrought iron, rain-soaked pavements, torn posters, graffiti messages… Any of these could inspire stitched textiles.

Observe and quickly sketch people as they move about and catch their social interaction – it takes practice, but it's worth the effort. Jot down words of description and feelings – create a story. Experiment with some of the ideas suggested below.

▶ *Spend a day in town with both camera and sketchbook to hand. Make sure you have adequate memory and a fully charged battery in your camera and venture into an unfamiliar area, for a fresher approach. Derelict walls, peeling paint, graffiti and torn posters can be as interesting as garden flowers. Images by the river, such as boats, complete with water reflections, could inspire watercolours; busy markets might be captured with a sketch in gouache.*

▶ *Consider industrial repeat patterns and shapes, including relationships with nature, such as the cobweb and the electricity pylon. Look at the negative shapes – the spaces in between.*

▶ *Perhaps this might be a good time to try some photo filters, for high-contrast shapes, or polarizing filters.*

Above: Inspirational patterns that make connections. Top to bottom: A billboard; an electricity pylon seen from below; early morning cobweb; Lift Bridge, Burlington. Right: **Time for a Rest (detail)** (Freda Surgenor, Australia).

Buildings – and architectural detail

Buildings, old and new, have always been a great source of inspiration for the artist. Reflections on glass, skyscrapers that reach for the sky, detail in carvings, the choice and colours of stone or any other new materials – all combine to make architecture a favourite subject. Buildings represent a culture and society, reflecting a people and their sense of design, whatever their age. Architectural detail can give us a sense of a bygone time, for example the ornate detail and intricate patterns of Victorian architecture which contrast with the smooth, clean lines of modern high-rise office blocks.

▶ *Look for images of doorways, arches, alleyways and windows as well as sculpture. Our observations are keener and we take more photos and read more about the history of architecture on holiday because what we see is not familiar. Hillside towns with pale ancient ruins or fishing villages with light and reflections might offer a chance to experiment with a new art medium.*

▶ *When photographing monuments or tall buildings, consider Photoshop Elements for the Transform tool, which can be used to straighten verticals in building walls.*

Above left: **Red Roofs** (Elizabeth Barton, USA). Above, top: Scottish rooftops with sharp contrasts in colour and shape. Above, bottom: Toronto high-rise showing reflections and pattern.

Still life

Still-life arrangements can contain any subject you choose, from the popular vase of flowers, bowl of fruit, glass of wine, bottle and/or bread and cheese to a favourite old pair of boots, an antique bowl or a sculptured head. Subjects from nature can be combined in an interesting composition – seed pods and different stages of a plant's life, with flower, pod and seed together... The list is endless.

In a still life, we make finite observations of colour, light and shade. It is always interesting to compare a sketch done from 'life' and the same view in a photograph. The former will may not have all the detail, but will exhibit more energy.

Placing of elements

The popular triangular composition is often used in still life: a line can be drawn from three focal points (not all of equal prominence) to create movement and keep the viewer moving around the surface area. Textile artists should employ these same principles in their own surface designs.

Still life is the easiest of all the themes with which to practise realism in drawing and painting. Gather an interesting assortment of subjects and when you are happy with a composition, check the light source for highlights and shadows. Take a few photographs from different angles so you can continue drawing when the light fades.

▶ *Consider more negative shapes – by working in black-and-white cut shapes you can see how elements work well within a frame of reference.*

Above, top: **The Vase of Roses** (Sandra Meech, UK). Coloured-pencil sketch.
Above: **Capsicums and Crystal** (Freda Surgenor, Australia). Triangular composition in watercolour and gouache. Above right: Pear compositions and seed pods to sketch.
Right: Negative elements within a frame.

Above: **Stills from a Life #22** (Dominie Nash, USA).

Left: **Pumpkin** (Freda Surgenor, Australia). Watercolour and gouache still life.

Right: **Shopping Again?**
(Jae Maries, UK). Textile art
that tells a story.

Drawing from life: portraits, the human figure and animals

Capturing a true likeness in a portrait takes practice, but quite it's achievable for the beginner. Portraiture has long offered a wonderful record of fashion and dress – a glimpse of a period in society. In the past, many artists only survived because the patronage of the aristocracy or the court allowed them the opportunity to experiment with and develop new materials.

The human figure takes more practice, and drawing from 'life', with a model posing, is the ultimate challenge. With some guidance, however, perhaps in a series of classes where there are short and long poses, it is possible for a beginner to achieve some good results. The clothed figure, which could be a friend or family member, offers a chance to look at folds and the pattern of fabric.

Animals can also be fun to draw and paint. They will not 'hold a pose' on demand, so it's best to use photographs, perhaps providing a lasting memory of a favourite pet or a chance to draw exotic animals or birds on holiday. Have you wondered how nature artists capture the image of the charging lion? Obviously, it's done with a camera.

The face and the human figure, as well as wild birds and animals, have long been interpreted in stitch, both in embroidery and in art quilts. It takes a measure of confidence, ability, design sense and good taste to make it work successfully, but everyone should have a go. Perhaps stylized faces could be worth a try (see page 36).

▶ *Quick sketches of people in public places (especially children) may be difficult, but it is easy to take photos these days. Just be aware of personal privacy.*

▶ *Use a family member, sitting comfortably in a studied pose, for some quick and long poses. Consider the light source and how the fabric drapes, and take a photo for a record.*

▶ *A self-portrait perhaps? Look at proportion in the face, breaking down elements for ease. If you use a mirror to sketch a head-and-shoulders portrait of yourself, you will be drawing the image in reverse, not how others see you. A photographic reference could be also used.*

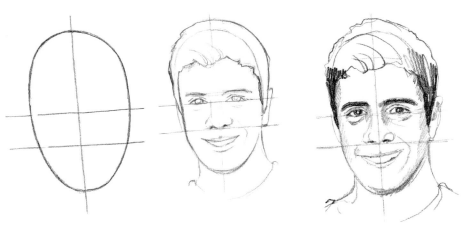

Top and middle right: Drawing from life takes practice; Quick line sketches in public. Right: **Portrait of Warren** (Sandra Meech, UK). Start with a simple head shape, then consider the placement of the eyes, nose and mouth as you build up the detail.

Above: **Seams Like Degas** (Lura Schwartz Smith, USA).
Realistic and beautifully executed fabric painting from
life. Right and far right: **Golden Hands** (full piece and
detail) (Lura Schwartz Smith, USA).

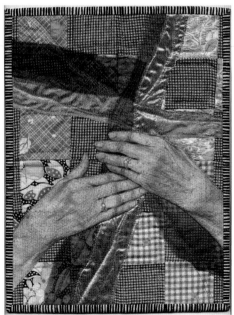

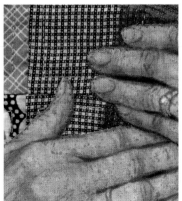

Collectibles and hobbies

Included in this review of subjects that can inspire is a still-life approach with ephemera or collectible items. Themes could include an eclectic range of pieces – jewellery, articles of costume and world textiles, fashion items (shoes for instance), musical instruments or garden tools... Anything goes!

Take the opportunity to draw or paint your pieces in several still-life compositions, considering pattern, colour and texture. Perhaps the subject could form the basis of an embellished mixed-media journal. With many more surface-design techniques available, motifs can be appliquéd, painted, stencilled or printed onto cloth with transferred photographs and writing included (see page 111 for more on photo imagery). Don't forget to consider other mixed-media materials such as beads, sequins and buttons for that added 'extra' (see chapter 5 for more mixed-media inspiration).

▶ *A group of objects from the past, memories from school, a piece of old jewellery, ticket stubs, baby shoes you couldn't throw away – all can be assembled into a pleasing composition. Take photos for reference as well as creating a sketch or two. This is a good time to write about memories and what these things mean – for future reference or just to help you remember.*

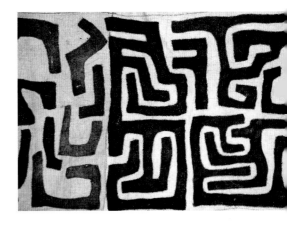

Above: This piece of Kuba cloth from central Africa, rich in pattern and texture, could provide inspiration.

Above: **Venetian Masks** (Kris Michael, Canada). The colour and shapes in this photograph would make a wonderful textile piece.

Right: **A Pair of Old Boots** (Sandra Meech, UK). I couldn't resist drawing them before they 'retired'. Soft pencil.

Above and right (detail): **Quilt Blog** (Sara Impey,
UK). Amazing stitch with an inspired message.

Social comment: the media, family and politics

Social or personal themes may be concept-based, exploring a deeper meaning or just telling an emotive story. Historically, many themes in art have been a response to politics or the social climate, but in many ways contemporary stitched-textile artists can go further. We see many themes based on issues such as the ravages of war, poverty, AIDS or women's health, as well as ecological themes such as global warming and hurricane damage. To balance this, there are also wonderful art quilts that express beauty, memories, family and fun. Words and writings are often included in textiles and they can inform and intrigue the viewer.

Consider posters as an art form as well as an advertising tool and reflect how they were used in wartime propaganda or how billboards can reinforce social thinking. The world of advertising is often a good place to look for design styles and the way a mixture of drawing, sketching and photography can be collaged together for dramatic effect.

▶ *Newspapers and magazines with social, environmental or political content can be gathered together for use in collage. Add your own words and views on the subject.*
▶ *Images of interesting billboards or a wall of torn posters offer layers of messages with different meanings that will definitely spark some ideas.*

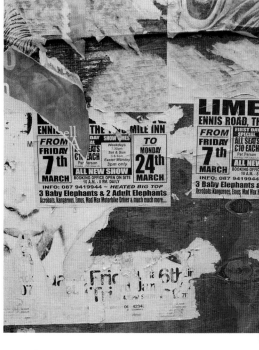

Above: **Limerick Posterwall** (Sandra Meech, UK).

Right: **Hunted** (Bente Vold Klausen, Norway). A dramatic target – painted and dyed art cloth.

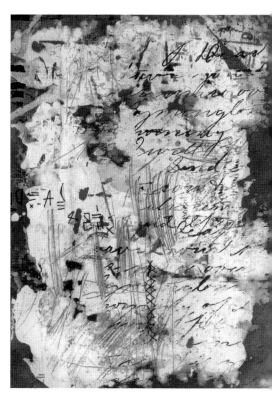

Above: **Three Letters (detail)** (Els van Baarle, Netherlands).

33

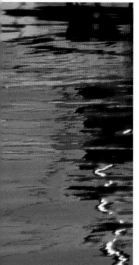

Taking a step into the abstract

Once we gain confidence in drawing, sketching and painting realistic subjects, we will quickly want to explore more abstract approaches. Many of the styles of abstract art adapt extremely well to being interpreted with fabric and stitch.

Abstract expressionism began when artists attempted to express attitudes and emotions in their work in a kind of spontaneous way, through non-representational means. The essence of the original subject was implied, but through exaggerated design and composition or use of colour, resulting in a painting that was more dynamic and emotionally charged.

Consider the Impressionist movement and how controversial artists such as Manet, Monet and later Picasso were perceived by the conventional art society. They seemed to have broken so many rules. Today, there are many creative approaches that we can learn from the world of art that translate well into today's contemporary stitched textiles. Sometimes, the approach is realistic and at other times the subject is less obvious or the concept is illustrated through colour, shape, pattern or movement.

Art galleries, containing the old masters as well as the most contemporary art, are still the best places to learn about art. Usually, photography is not permitted, so always take a small sketchbook for ideas. Look at the obvious – the design, colour, composition and use of media – as well as the emotion and vitality conveyed with each brushstroke, or the concept behind the theme. This contemplation can inspire creative avenues and the stitch choices we need to make for our future 'journey' in textiles.

- *Consider a favourite photo and abstract and enlarge four or five different sections, offering a range of shapes. Rotate or flip them for a different dynamic.*
- *Flattened perspective is another popular way of abstracting a realistic still-life composition. Often used for subjects on a table, it seems to invite you into the picture.*

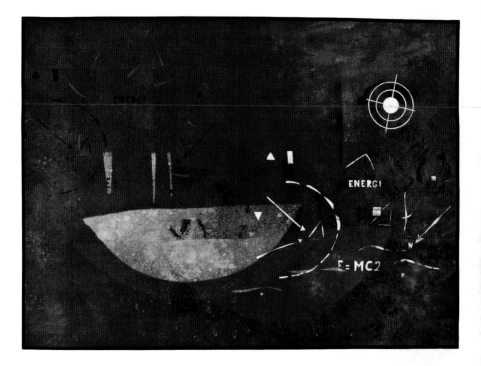

Above: Reykjavik harbour boats. One image abstracted in five different ways that could inspire a new design. Right: **The Eternal Journey** (Bente Vold Klausen, Norway). Opposite: **Fugue XI (detail)** (Sue Benner, USA).

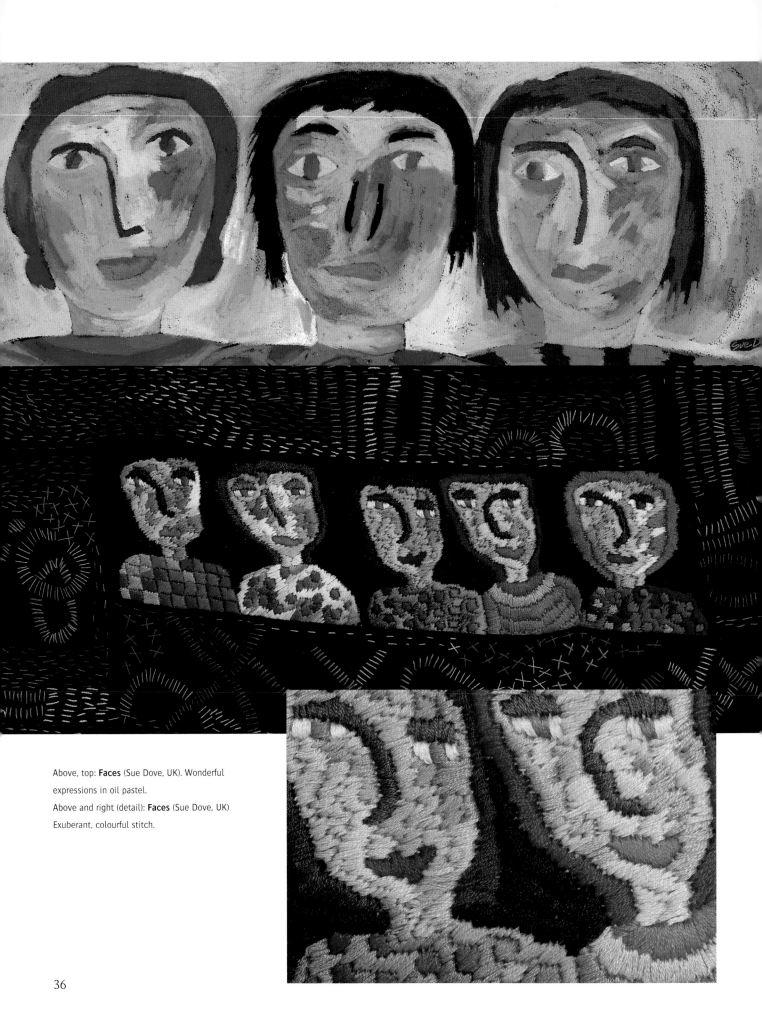

Above, top: **Faces** (Sue Dove, UK). Wonderful
expressions in oil pastel.
Above and right (detail): **Faces** (Sue Dove, UK)
Exuberant, colourful stitch.

2

DRAW, SKETCH AND STITCH

From the beginning, man has made 'marks' somewhere in his environment, from cave paintings and cup-and-ring symbols in stone to hieroglyphics on ancient tomb walls. These marks provide a vast amount of information, including everyday life in the landscape, social observation and stories that identify man's existence. Such marks, including language and number symbols, give us a glimpse of what life was like thousands of years ago.

From the moment we are able to hold a pencil, we want to make marks. As children, it is second nature to want to scribble on anything with free abandon and it is this energy that we are desperate to find again as adults. A focus on drawing and sketching is perhaps one of the most important art techniques to practise, because the final stage of that pieced, layered or embroidered textile is essentially held together and embellished with stitch 'marks'.

If your stitching is to be exciting, confident sketching and drawing should come first. Relax and have fun practising drawing skills regularly – it will get easier each time. There will be familiar techniques and materials on offer, but working through the exercises with a choice of different subjects will offer countless challenges to explore. The illustrations are only suggestions – it is up to you to work through your own subjects and the references in the different exercises. Consider working with line on paper at the same time as trying out ideas on cloth and get used to making that connection between art and stitch.

Left: Rust rock found by the shore in county Mayo (Sandra Meech, UK).

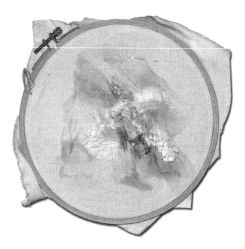

Above: **Ice Stitch** (Sandra Meech, UK). Watercolour pencil and wash on fabric.

Above: **Rune Stone** (Sandra Meech, UK). Pen and ink sketch. Below: Materials for sketching.

Materials

Listed here are basic art materials to have on hand for drawing, painting and sketching – you may have many already.

Papers and boards

- **Paper** comes in a vast variety of whites and soft colours and in different textures and weights, 90 gsm (grams per square metre) being thin and 300gsm being heavier.
- **Sketchbooks** Spiral and bound styles work best if paper is acid-free sized (to take wash better), white or cream cartridge, at least 140gsm in weight. Remember that painting some sketchbook pages in advance with a light wash can make them seem less intimidating. Use dilute watercolour or Brusho paint. An A5 (8 × 5in) landscape shape will be good for many of the exercises to follow.
- **Cartridge** is the cheapest and most common paper; it has a fairly smooth surface that can take wet and dry media.
- **Pastel papers** have more texture. Ingres paper is the most popular and provides a tinted background.
- **Board** Bristol (CS2) or other smooth mounting boards will provide a firm background.
- **Black-coated scraperboard** can be used to create scratched sgraffito detail.

Dry and wet media

- **Pencils** of good quality, from F (hard) to HB, 3B, and 6B (soft) – look for superior wood casing; mechanical pencils could also be included.
- **Graphite stick** Solid lead, sometimes coated, it can be used on its side for tone.
- **Erasers** Kneaded erasers leave no residue; white plastic erasers will also protect paper.
- **Craft knife** Best with disposable retractable blades; surgical scalpels can be used with care (have a cork protection for the blade).
- **Charcoal and conté pencils** and sticks also run from hard F to 4B (also include a white conté pencil for highlights).
- **Paper and rubber stump** or cotton bud, for softening and blending.
- **Markers and fibre-tipped pens** These should include a fine-line roller, technical and art-pen varieties, as well as coloured pens.
- **Calligraphy pens** with a few thick and thin or cartoon-style interchangeable nibs, to be used with india ink.
- **Coloured pencils** You will need a wide variety; types include chalk pencils, conté pencils, wax pencils and water-soluble ones.
- **Wax coloured pencils** provide a great variety of colours, as well as hard and soft types for blending and toning.
- **Chalk pastels** also come in a wide range of types, from soft and hard pastels to pencils.
- **Oil pastels** come in a great selection of colours and include Markal Paintstiks.
- **China markers** in white are useful for highlights and provide a fine tip.
- **White candle** is used for resists.

- **Waterproof inks** or liquid acrylic inks can be used with a fine brush, dip or quill pens, sponges or sticks.
- **Brusho** is a powder dye, similar to ink; mixed with water, it can be thickened for use as fine line.
- **Solvents and mediums** can be used with oils as well as oil pastels on paper.

For using on cloth

- **ChromaCoal** These black and coloured sticks are first used on white cloth then heat set.
- **Fine and thicker permanent pens** can be used on tightly woven smooth fabric; if you draw on polyester sateen first, and then apply colour with disperse transfer dyes, this can provide interesting results.
- **Watercolour pencils and aquarelle sticks** will work on cotton and offer a background for stitch, but are not colourfast.
- **Oil pastels** can be used for rubbings on cloth that can then be heat set.
- **Thickened transfer dyes** can be used for drawings on paper that are heat-transferred onto polyesters and sized cottons.
- **Bleach pens** will discharge colour from dyed cloth.
- **Scraping tools or cut cardboard** can also provide line marks.
- **Freezer paper** is used as a stabilizer for cotton being fed through a printer and for generally finer line drawing on fabric.
- **Inkjet transfer papers** can be used with drawings on paper, scanned and printed with an inkjet, and then heat transferred.

Above: **Ornamental Cabbage** (Sandra Meech, UK). Permanent pen and ChromaCoal on stabilized cotton.

Below: Sketching pens and pencils.

39

For stitch drawings

- **Thin wadding (batting)** can be used for machine and hand samples; types include heavy sew-in Vilene (Pellon) interfacing, thin felt, domette, Thermore Light, needle punch or curtain linings.
- **Sewing machine** with an assortment of basic and embroidery thread and the essential darning foot. Basic feet for straight and zigzag stitch are also essential.
- **Hand-stitch** sewing kit, including scissors, embroidery needles, chenille needles and an 18.5/20cm (7/8 in) diameter hoop, if preferred, for smaller work.
- **Textures** for couching, such as textured wools, scrims, ribbons and threads.
- **Stranded or perle cottons** for hand stitches.
- **Needles** Embroidery and chenille needles of various sizes, and pins for general use.

Above: **Arctic Ice** (Sandra Meech, UK).

Below: **Shoreline** (Sandra Meech, UK).

Using line and tone

Line is the single most important link between art and stitch. Either line, shape, colour, texture, design or imagery can dominate the surface, but it is the way we handle stitched lines that will make the surface come to life. The drawn line is a vehicle for creative ideas, to record observations on paper or to document our feelings. Line is everywhere and a dynamic connecting thread between art and stitch.

Line will be practised throughout, from landscape, through detail in nature, to buildings, people and abstract forms. Every time you see line in your own work or in an art gallery, think of stitch. Making the connection between line and stitch will become easier and easier as you practise.

Pencil

Exploring types of pencils is the first step – simple hard and soft line, building up tone, adding texture, erasing and smudging.

- ▶ *First, take an HB, 2B, 4B, a very soft 6B pencil, a graphite stick and a charcoal pencil and make lines, cross-hatching, parallel lines and stippling to see how each creates a different effect.*
- ▶ *Build up tone by smudging with your finger, a pressed-paper tool or cotton bud.*
- ▶ *Create texture with a combination of line, smudging and erasing.*

Exercises using pencil

These are meant to be short experimental compositions and, although a subject is suggested, any theme is possible. You can use sketching paper or you might want to record some experiments directly into a sketchbook. Remember that these explorations in drawing and sketching are for your eyes only. Sometimes, these art exercises lead directly to fabric and stitch, so be prepared to move from one discipline to another if you feel so inspired.

- ▶ *Try one-minute drawings – take a favourite photo, focus on one part and do a small sketch. Time yourself!*

Above: Experiments with marks using soft pencil, including shading, erasing and smudging.

Hint
Paint sketchbook pages first before you do drawing exercises: it will make the blank space seem less intimidating.

Above: **Harvest** (Sandra Meech, UK). Charcoal sketch made in Scotland.

Above: Impressing a flower shape.

▶ *Try a simple landscape in your sketchbook, using line, tone and hatching for depth. Remember that looking through a camera lens or aperture card will offer good practice in isolating what you want to draw.*

▶ *Learn about impressing – put newspaper on the bottom (to take the impression) and cartridge on top; cover with tracing paper, and you are now ready to sketch. Using an HB pencil, draw a piece of fruit or a vegetable. Take away the drawing, making sure there is a clear impression and, with a soft pencil, shade over the drawing. You could also do this with a coloured pencil, using it to add a little colour.*

▶ *Take a favourite subject and create several studies, including details, to fill a sketchbook page. Shells, rocks, twigs and leaves all make good subjects.*

The 'Art Classes' throughout this book will enable you to delve deeper into a medium or further develop a personal theme. There are no time limits – just enjoy exploring the different suggestions. Connecting the art practice with stitch will become more obvious as you work through the book.

Hints

- Don't use a ruler if you can help it.
- Use thick and thin lines to create a slight shadow to create the illusion of dimension.

- For a symmetrical shape, such as a bottle or vase, a vertical half image can be drawn, and then traced. Flip over the tracing; draw the line from the back over the missing half, and the full shape will appear.

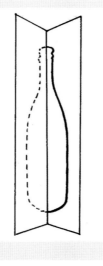

Above: **Shadow Walk** (Sandra Meech, UK).
Sketchbook page in charcoal.
Right: Scrunched-paper exercises.

42

Art Class 1
Layer, scrunch, fold and draw

Layer different types of paper – newspaper, magazine, cartridge, tracing, aluminium foil, textured paper and a page of writing. Scrunch them together so the different materials show. Take photos from different angles for a record, looking at light and shade. Using soft pencil, sketch what you see.

- Scan your photo into the computer and enlarge it, focusing on different areas – create several images.
- A black-and-white print will show how your line has been broken down, with added texture. Continue to enlarge the drawing to discover interesting effects that could relate to a final stitched piece.
- Don't forget that sketching in black and white is a good way to practise tonal values, and work with expressive line without the worry of mixing colour.

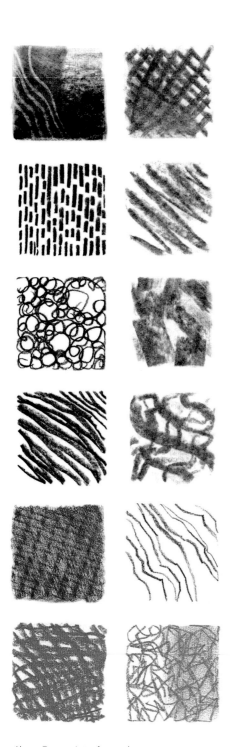

Charcoal, conté sticks and pencils

Charcoal and conté sticks are expressive materials that respond to more fluid movements as well as pressure. The sticks can be used on their sides or on the point. Building up tonal values can create very strong intense feeling on the surface. Sketching in black or sepia brown is a particularly good for drawing portraits and the human form.

▶ *With a charcoal or conté stick have fun with line, varying thicknesses and pressure, and creating parallel, cross-hatching and textural effects.*
▶ *Try mark-making with a brown conté pencil – a favourite medium for portraits.*
▶ *With a charcoal stick on its side, make some thick overlapping marks.*
▶ *Work from black to light with wide strokes, and blend the marks with your finger, a paper stump or a cotton bud.*
▶ *Use various erasers to create different line effects.*

Exercises in charcoal and conté

▶ *Try the same examples with conté as you did with charcoal or pencil, adding different textural effects. Don't forget to smudge for tone and use the erasing tools for marks in 'reverse'.*
▶ *Consider a landscape with distant mountains in mist: create the same effect in charcoal or with a conté stick.*
▶ *Draw a simple subject, such as a shell, in charcoal, and then smudge areas for shadow and tone. Marks and light areas are created by lifting out tone with an eraser.*

On fabric

ChromaCoal is a material very similar to conté, but it can be heat fixed onto cotton and stitched. Experiment with a small piece of cotton, ironed onto freezer paper for stability, then heat set. This might be good for shading areas on an art quilt.

Above: Try a variety of examples using charcoal and conté and see the difference.
Right: Try a still-life study with brown or sepia conté pencil.
The two right-hand images, of a misty landscape and a barn window, were created in charcoal with pen-line accents.

Art Class 2
Tonal collage

Using charcoal and rubbing it onto tracing paper, create a tonal collage with five or six densities (tones) of black and grey on the paper. Using a still-life reference, either taken from a photo or direct from life (perhaps a vase of flowers or bowl of fruit), tear and stick together a composition. Later, marks can be made by scraping with a knife blade. To prevent smudging, you may want to use a fixative at different stages before gluing the sections down.

Repeat this exercise with a portrait. The polarizing filter in Photoshop Elements gives you the option of breaking a black-and-white portrait photo into four or five sections.

On fabric

These techniques could become an abstract still-life composition, made with dyed or patterned fabrics in black, white, grey and cream (off-white neutrals). Perhaps some colour in stitch could be added for interest. Remember to use thin batting for small fabric collages.

Top: Vase of tulips. Below left: A posterized version of the image; drawing with charcoal tracing-paper sections; detail of finished piece with accents. Below: Tonal tulip collage.

Above: Line examples, including parallel lines, cross-hatching, pointillism... anything goes!

Pens and markers

Markers, felt tip and roller ink art pens have transformed sketching and drawing. Making fine, medium or thick lines, many patterns, textures and tones can be created – cross-hatching lines, parallel lines, dot tones and scribble tones. **Always remember that a line makes the closest connection to stitch.**

▶ *Try ballpoints, fibre-tip pens, markers, brush pens, mechanical-style pens, permanent pens... anything you have to hand. Create as many variations of tone, line and texture as you can with cross-hatching lines, parallel lines, dot tones and scribble tones. Consider varying the thickness of line and the spacing to reflect depth, shadow or tone.*
▶ *Repeat with some of the pen studies and add water for a wash effect.*
▶ *Fill a sheet of letterhead paper with at least 12 different boxes of line examples, including the ones illustrated on the left.*
▶ *A favourite pen is the calligraphy pen with a nib that will give you a thick or thin line (cartoonists use this); this pen creates a very organic line that can be achieved very easily and is good for sketches and quick still-life or landscape drawings.*

Exercises

▶ *Try a simple sketch of people in public – don't be too critical with yourself. Practise seeing and observing. Fill a sketchbook page with lots of little overlapping sketches in pen line. Don't feel embarrassed about sketching in public places.*

Hint

Photos might be easy reference as well. Allow extra time on the next occasion you are at the train station or shopping, but be aware of security areas where no photography is allowed.

Above: A quick sketch with a calligraphy pen and ink.

Above: **Sheep**. Drawn with a combination of pen and pencil for soft shading.

Right: **The Other Side of the Lake #2 (detail)** (Dorothy Caldwell, Canada).

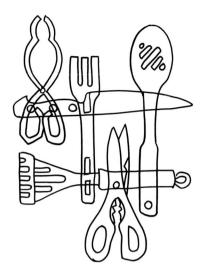

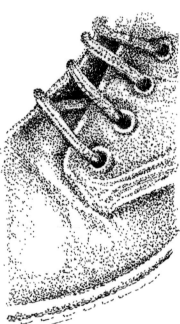

Above left: Kitchen utensils in fibre-pen line. Above: Negative compositions taken from photos with the black and white areas equally balanced.
Far left: **Bowl** (Sandra Meech, UK). Pen and pastel on Ingres paper. Left: Boot detail in a pointillist style.

Right: Sketchbook landscape with pen and charcoal. Don't forget to go back to your favourite scenes and create a new sketch in a different medium.

Left: **Sara and Emil** (Charlotte Yde, Denmark).
A wonderful machine-stitch sketch based on an
edited photo and computer sewing software.
Below: the boot detail shown on the opposite page
has been enlarged and transferred onto fabric for
stitching with French knots.

▶ *Kitchen utensils or garden tools can be arranged and drawn in pen. Keep adding to
the collection.*

▶ *Perhaps a small animal study or detail of a feather or fur pattern might be the next
step to take.*

▶ *Create a section of an earlier pencil drawing in pointillist dots, paying attention to
light and shade. Dots are larger and set closer together for deeper tones and smaller
and further apart for light areas.*

▶ *Take a look at Photoshop filters – 'artistic' effects include outline, sketching and
posterizing.*

On fabric

▶ *Freehand or traced drawings and writings using both fine and thicker permanent
pens can be also done on any smooth white or dyed fabrics that have been stabilized
with freezer paper. Polyester sateen with a matt surface takes permanent marker pens
and could later be coloured with transfer dyes (see page 76) or overlaid with sheers
and colourful stitch added. These surfaces become a mixed-media approach and
should not be machine washed.*

▶ *Use a particular section of the pointillist drawing and recreate it in French knots,
stitched by hand.*

Remember that you can experiment with many of the exercises over and over again,
taking a different subject each time.

Above: Icebergs in marker on stabilized cotton.
Sheers and stitch could be added.

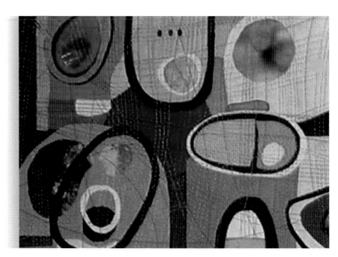

Above and right (detail): **Urban
Landscape** (Bethan Ash, UK). Hand-dyed
and painted fabric, improvisationally
cut, fused and stitched.
Opposite page, top: **Red Morning**
(Elizabeth Barton, USA).

Art Class 3
Building detail in line and tone

Buildings, old and new, are a favourite subject for stitched-textile artists. Whether it is buildings seen on travels to distant places or the urban cityscape in the nearest town, architecture offers great possibilities for drawing and sketching.

• Create a line drawing from a detail from a photograph of an interesting building. Consider using black, dense areas to reflect shadow and record sculptural detail.

• Another drawing of a group of buildings could include black line with a sepia ink or coloured wash.

On fabric
A black-and-white line drawing could be printed onto heat-transfer paper then ironed onto pale fabric with sheers, appliquéd fabrics and stitch added. Work small to create a mini series.

Above: A line drawing in pen. Left: Launceston from a distance in pen with sepia ink wash.

51

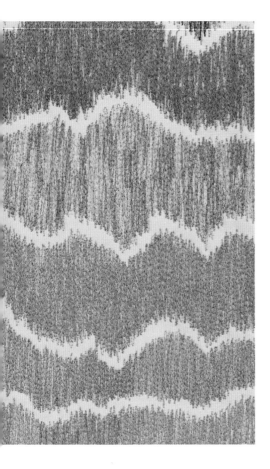

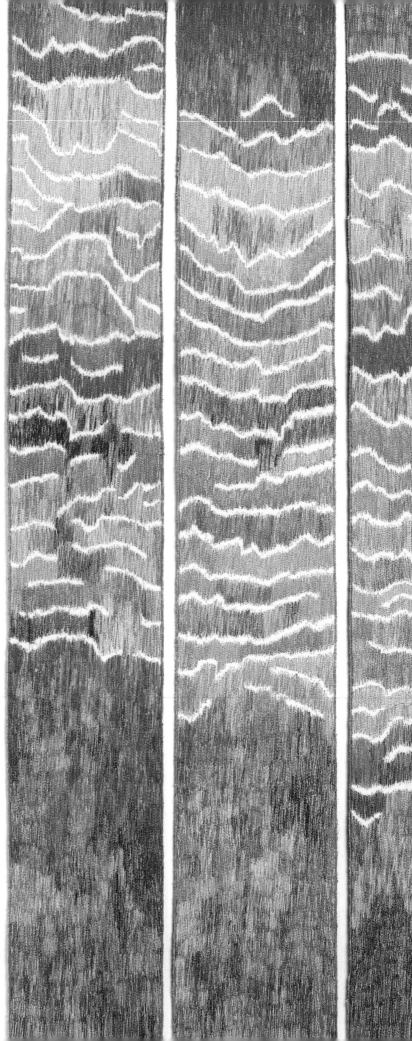

Right and above (detail): **Aurora**
(Dirkje van der Horst Beetsma, Netherlands).
Vigorous machine-stitch marks convey the
shimmering colour of the aurora.

Art Class 4
Still life in black and white

Possible subjects for your still life could be a bowl of fruit, a vase of flowers or any detail in nature: when you choose a subject, pay attention to line and tone. For one of the drawings consider negative spaces, keeping some areas white.

Above: Cowslip bouquet – the original image.

Landscape in black and white

Using sgraffito ways of scratching out line on a black inked surface, we can see how the stalks of winter harvest can look in line. India ink is painted onto card stock and scratched back with a knife blade. This effect has been effectively used in machine stitch on fabric applications.

To work on fabric:

- Enlarge a detail from any line drawing done so far and try to replicate it in a freehand machine stitch. Perhaps varying the width of the stitch (satin stitch) or colour of the thread could be interesting.
- Use a bleach pen or fill a small plastic dispenser with bleach and draw on black discharge cotton. (Work in a ventilated room and wear a mask.)
- Take a section of the sgraffito landscape and replicate its lines with hand stitch in coloured cottons.

Top: Simple line drawing. Middle: The finished sketch. Bottom: Wild tundra flowers in black line with negative areas.

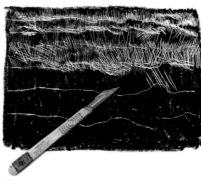

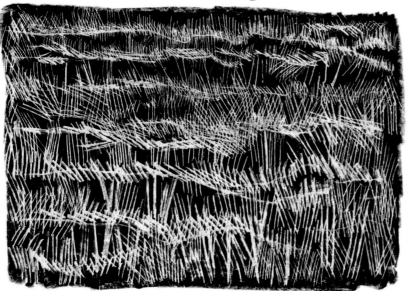

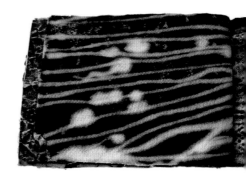

Top left: Harvest reference photo and prepared inked card. Left: finished sgraffito picture with vigorous lines that could inspire stitch by hand or machine. Above: bleach on black discharge cotton.

Above: **Iceland Lava Fields**
(Sandra Meech, UK). Stark images
of growth in a black desert.

Above, top: **Travelling to Mungo**
(Sandra Meech, UK). Coloured-pencil sketch
on painted pages. Above: **Walls of China**
(Sandra Meech, UK). Sketch.

Right: **Aerial Ice Flow** (Sandra Meech, UK).
In this sketch, I used a monochromatic
approach for extra impact.

Coloured pencils

Coloured pencils offer immediate results on paper. Because they are portable they are a favourite medium for sketchbooks, and there are many varieties and colours to choose from. Soft, blendable varieties are best for overlapping colour, and watercolour styles work well for soft landscapes. All pencils with strong rich colour are good for creating bold shapes and pattern. The more colours you have to choose from the better.

Basic techniques

▶ *Try some of the line and tone exercises done earlier with coloured pencils, varying the texture and blending colour.*

▶ *Learn to burnish colours to create a depth and shine. Any colour can be combined with white, grey or yellow, or worked with a paper stump. The textural line of the pencil is lost and the colour will be intense. Try scratching back detail with a knife blade (this works best if the paper is smooth).*

▶ *Water-soluble pencils can offer a better connection with fabric, as the wash effects could be recreated with sheers. These can be used as a base for hand stitching and, although not as colourfast as dyes, can become a starting point for a stitch sample.*

Exercises for coloured pencil

▶ *Using a red and green apple or colourful pear as a subject, create a full-colour sketch in pencils with only three colours – two reds (scarlet and crimson), two yellows (lemon and golden yellow) and two blues (cyan and cool cobalt blue). Carefully blended, these can be used for every colour needed and all of them combined make brownish black.*

▶ *Working in a horizontal A5 (8 x 5in) sketchbook (with previously painted pages), recreate a detail from nature with pen and coloured pencils.*

▶ *Use watercolour pencils for line and wash– choose clean bright colours, based on a subject such as a sample of textile or a fashion or costume detail. Concentrate on pattern, paying attention to folds in the fabric (light and shade).*

▶ *Taking at least two sketchbook spreads, fill them with line and coloured pencil illustrations taken from favourite photographs. (Paint a very pale wash on one of the spreads.)*

▶ *On smooth paper, create a study, perhaps an animal drawing, with coloured pencil. Use an eraser to lighten and scratch back lines with a knife for more details of fur. This technique could be used for any subject.*

▶ *On fabric, try a coloured-pencil wash on an open-weave white cotton for experimental purposes, but this is not lightfast. It could, however, become the background for machine marks, couched materials or hand stitching. Take a section from a coloured-pencil exercise and adapt this to fabric with coloured threads, stitching by machine.*

Above: Coloured-pencil exercise using three colours. Below: **Sketchbook Oz** – detail of the red cap gum flower and seed.

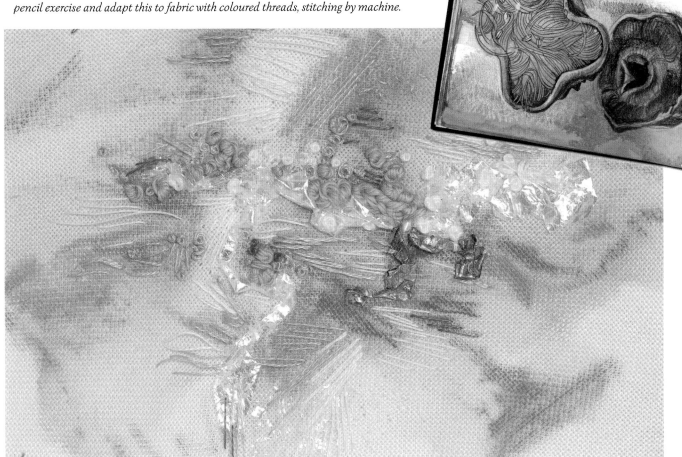

Above: **Ice Thaw** (Sandra Meech, UK). Coloured-pencil wash on open-weave cotton with embroidery stitch.

55

Above: **Jokulsarlon Spring Thaw**
(Sandra Meech, UK). Oil pastel on black
fabric, heat-fixed with machine stitch.

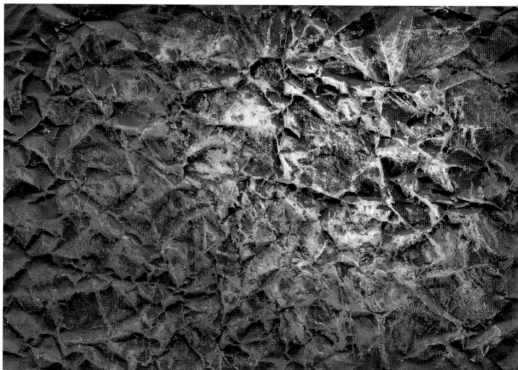

Right: Oil pastels rubbed onto
scrunched black paper.

Oil and chalk pastels, sticks and pencils

Not only do chalks and oil pastels give interesting lines, but they can also create wonderful surface textures on paper that can mimic fabric. Colours can be strong or subtle, depending on the subject, and can be blended easily using a paper stump, brush or finger. Chalk is only useful for fine art applications and you will need a fixative at different stages of use as it smudges easily. Oil pastels translate very well on paper, in sketchbooks and on fabric; some varieties are water soluble for wash effects. A set of 24 would be a good investment.

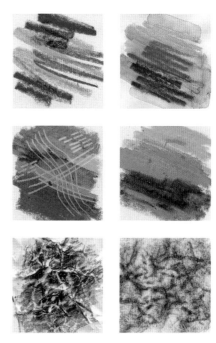

Above: Oil pastels layered, as a wash, scratched back, blended, and rubbed on crinkled paper and stabilized cotton.

▶ *For mark-making, try any of the previous exercises with a range of colours in oil pastels. Do the same with chalks and chalk pencils.*
▶ *Use the pastel on its side, creating textured papers and overlapping colours.*
▶ *Intensely overlay colours and scratch back for sgraffito line detail.*
▶ *Media such as solvents can be used to allow pastels to blend more easily.*
▶ *Soft chalks in large or small round sticks or pastel pencils can be used for sketchbook work. Try using pencils on a mid-tone Ingres paper for a museum subject, with colour, light and shade.*
▶ *Shavings of children's wax crayons can be ironed (cover with parchment first) on white paper; next, a watercolour or Brusho (see page 85) wash is laid over this to create an inspirational surface for a future textile piece.*

Exercises

▶ *With a still-life shape – a jug, a vase or some flowers, for instance – overlap the colour on paper and scratch back detail with a sharp knife (the sgraffito technique).*
▶ *Scrunch black paper and apply oil pastel (on its side) on the top of the fold for marble-like effects.*
▶ *Oil pastel marks on fabric can be fixed with heat. Also available in pearlized and metallic colours, Markal-style sticks require 24 hours to dry before heat fixing.*
▶ *Consider using oil pastel on paper or cloth to take rubbings off a textured surface.*

A collagraph was the textured surface used in the example illustrated left.

Hint
Remember to look at computer programs like Paint Shop Pro or Photoshop Elements for artistic effects in oil and chalk pastel. Any sketch or image can easily be transferred onto cloth for stitch (see page 111).

Left: Rubbing with oil pastel onto a textured collagraph (see page 120). Above: Museum sketch on Ingres paper with pen line and chalk pastel.

Above: **Northland (detail)** (Sandra Meech, UK). Pencil sketch inspired by the work of Tom Thomson.

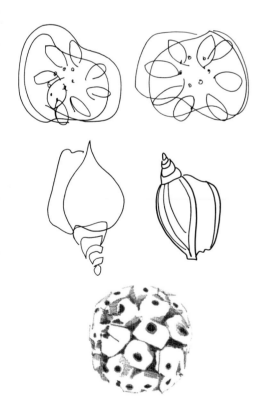

Above, top to bottom: Spontaneous quick sketches without looking then observing; still life worked quickly on cloth.

Art Class 5
Art as inspiration

Taking just a small section of an impressionist painting (consider Seurat, van Gogh or Monet), and without worrying about copying it exactly, try to capture the essence or mood and the colour choices of the painting in coloured pencils. My example is a painting by Tom Thomson, a well-known Canadian landscape artist, from which I copied a section in coloured pencil. It is also possible to get great results with oil pastel on brown parcel paper, creating the effect of how fine artists paint with oils on wood.

Experiments on fabric
• Translate the colour and energetic brushstrokes from your illustration by applying coloured fabric to a ground fabric, using fabric glue or backing pieces with Bondaweb and heat setting them in place. Deal with the background first before adding the middle and foreground detail.
• Don't forget that oil pastel can be drawn directly onto cotton, covered with baking parchment and heat fixed. Perhaps it would be good to try a small section first.
• Have fun with free-machine stitching across the surface, perhaps adding hand-stitched marks for emphasis.

Exploring spontaneity

We can sometimes get obsessive about the accuracy of our sketched observations. It is important to remember that happy accidents often occur and something fresh and vital happens that was not planned. There is always room for working through line in a serendipitous way, such as tossing pick-up sticks in the air to see how they land, closing your eyes and drawing shapes for memory, or making 'marks' inspired by words of emotion. Such marks are less consciously done, but they are nevertheless just as valid as a well-executed line. Some of the intuitive art exercises below may be liberating and worth a try in any art materials at hand.

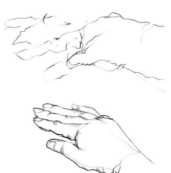

▶ *Words of inspiration – fold a letterhead-sized page into six squares. Keep a blue, a red and a black pencil crayon nearby and randomly choose (pull them out of a hat) five of the following words – COLD, HOT, LOVE, HATE, CONFUSED, FREE, HOPE, GROW – creating your own word (based on a personal theme or emotional connection) for the sixth. Without looking, use each word to fill one of the squares with marks.*
▶ *Draw your own hand, first in soft pencil without looking at it, then again while looking and observing. The first drawing is free and abandoned and the second more controlled.*

Above: Hands drawn with and without looking.

Right: **Northland** (Sandra Meech, UK). Image transfer from sketch with applied fabric.

Above: Interpretive stitch drawing by machine.

▶ *Left-brain or mirror drawing – draw something just from its reflection, backwards or even upside down.*

▶ *Looking at something simple in front of you, machine stitch without looking. Keep your fingers as far away from the embroidery foot as possible (only try this if you are competent in machine stitching). Alternatively, study a section of a photograph you have taken, and then put it away and try to draw it with the needle on white or cream fabric.*

▶ *You can also have interpretive fun machine stitching to the rhythm and beat of music.*

Art Class 6
Moving marks

From a standing position, use a long stick or a small sponge applicator (taped onto a thin piece of wood or bamboo) dipped into black acrylic ink. Make 'marks' on a large A1-sized (22 x 34in) sheet of white cartridge paper on the floor. Use movement from the shoulder to create lines and shapes inspired by a theme, such as waves; use rhythm, jagged lines, dot marks or just have some fun with pattern. Sections of this could suggest an abstract composition.

• Photograph sections to be used later to develop a design or composition.
• Look at any interesting shapes, including positive and negative areas.
• Play with positive and negative shapes in Photoshop Elements and change the colours for fun.
• Print a number of black-and-white photocopies for colouring with wash, coloured pencil or oil pastel for inspiration.

Remember that a thick or thin line on its own is a 'mark' and can be either flat or dimensional. As it joins itself, it becomes a shape and shapes can be distorted, repeated or flipped for a more dynamic result. With line, anything goes!

Above: These marks are vigorous and spontaneous. Right: An isolated section is reversed black and white and digitally coloured.

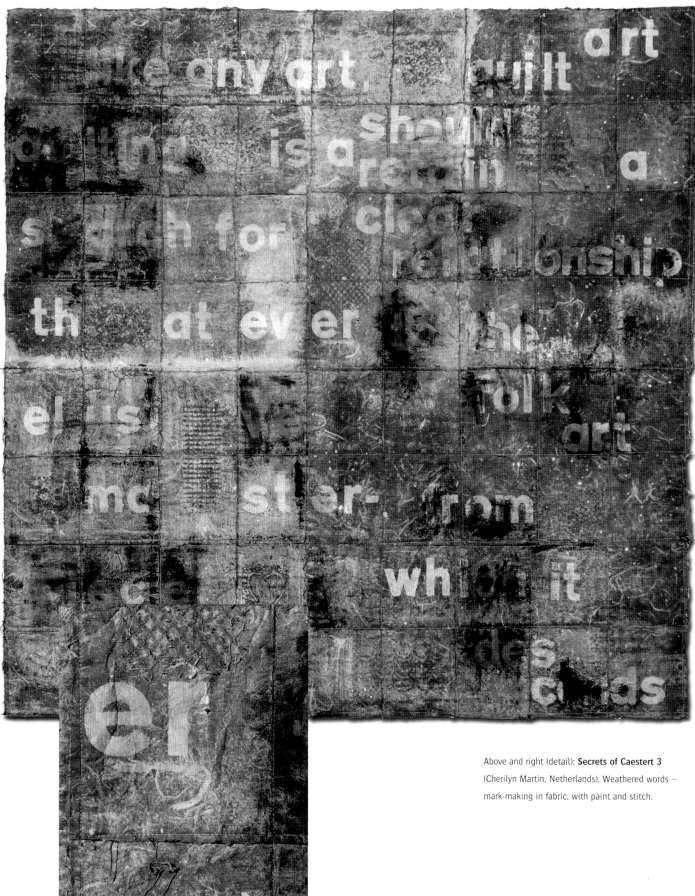

Above and right (detail): **Secrets of Caestert 3**
(Cherilyn Martin, Netherlands). Weathered words –
mark-making in fabric, with paint and stitch.

COLOUR

Colour is all around us and provides artists and everyone in stitched textiles with a limitless source of inspiration. It communicates so much – setting the mood, with individual colours awaking deeper meanings or eliciting a dynamic emotional response from the viewer.

Isaac Newton first studied the properties of white light as it broke down into the spectrum we all know – red, orange, yellow, green, blue, indigo and violet. Artists such as Matisse, Hundertwasser, Dufy and Miró, to name a few, constantly influence choices in textile art. For many textile artists – as for painters – colour can be the main stimulus for their 'art'.

Photography can play a wonderful role in capturing colour detail and mood at any time of day or in any season, providing us with a record to use over and over again. Sometimes, a subtle or minimal use of colour or monochrome can create a more powerful message than a full-colour scene.

No review of art practice would be complete without revisiting colour theory. In stitched textiles, we are familiar with the colour wheel and might be confident using and choosing colour for our work. But mixing and using colour in art with different media (coloured pencils, oil pastels, watercolour, gouache, acrylics or oils) is different from working with fabric. The best way to understand colour theory is to mix pigments yourself with each type of media; you will find that the results will be slightly different, according to the medium. To keep it simple, the examples on page 64 are done with gouache paint, which is an opaque easy-to-mix water-soluble medium, often used like watercolours, for illustration and painting.

Above: **Kantha Houses** (Lynn Creighton, UK). Left: **Fugue VIII (detail)** (Sue Benner, USA). A wonderful juxtaposition of colour, movement and pattern. Dye and paint on silk and cotton, monoprinted, fused and machine-quilted.

Above left and right: Colour charts with two yellows and two reds and two reds and two blues.

Above: Perfect colour combinations in nature.

You should use at least two each of the primary colours in order to create the best choice of secondary and tertiary colours. If each of these primary colours includes a cool and a warm hue, every shade can be obtained.

• Lemon yellow and cadmium yellow
• Cadmium red and alizarin crimson
• Cobalt blue and cerulean blue

Secondary colours are the oranges, greens and purples blended from the warm and cool primaries.

Tertiary colours are the colours mixed from adjacent secondary colours on the colour wheel. When using the cool and warm primaries, you can achieve a huge selection of colours.

Other important colours that are added to every palette are brown – burnt sienna, burnt umber – Payne's grey, lamp black and titanium white. Greens – viridian green and hooker's green – are often bought separately.

Using a medium that you already have – perhaps gouache or watercolour – work through some mixing exercises. Many of these exercises can be painted directly onto sized sketch paper for your own record. A landscape-shaped sketchbook, for mixing experiments, drawing exercises and small sketches to follow, would become a good reference.

Hint

Remember – this palette will provide a complete range of colours for most media. You could start simply with just the warm and cool primaries and then add black and white. Student-quality paints are perfectly adequate for a first try.

Basic colour exercises

For these exercises, you will need the following:

- A small set of gouache or watercolours with basic primaries – two yellow, two red, two blue – plus black and white.
- Three sable or imitation sable brushes, sizes 1, 3 and 5.
- Sheets of sized white cartridge sketch paper or a landscape-shaped bound or spiral sketchbook.

Colour-mixing exercises

▶ *Blend the primaries together – the examples above contain two yellows and two reds, two reds and two blues, and two yellows with two blues. You can see how different the results are.*

▶ *Blend a primary and its complementary colour together – add red to green, orange to blue or purple to yellow.*

▶ *Add a touch of white to any colour to create a tint and some black or Payne's grey to create a shade.*

▶ *Optically mix two primaries together to resemble the pointillist style of Impressionist painters such as George Seurat. This technique could be conveyed on cloth with seeding stitch or French knots.*

▶ *Consider analogous colour combinations in nature and try to capture the colours you can see with paint on paper. Analogous colours are three to four adjacent colours on the colour wheel with a touch of the vibrant colour opposite. An example of an analogous colour sequence could be green–turquoise–blue with a touch of bright orange.*

Above left and right: Chart with two yellows and two blues; chart with red to green, yellow to purple, white to blue, and orange to grey.

Above: This landscape photograph, taken in County Mayo, perfectly shows the greyed purple family of colours mixed with golden yellow.

▶ *Isolate a 2.5cm (1in) section from a favourite photograph and enlarge the area to 15cm (6in) and blend colours in gouache to match the photograph. Don't worry if the detail isn't particularly accurate: it is only a colour exploration. Consider the neutral colours – beige, grey and brown – which calm the vibrant dynamic colours you have chosen.*

▶ *Look at colour combinations from sections of your own photographs and look at how colour rules apply.*

▶ *Play with colour, using Photoshop Elements or Paint Shop Pro – here (left), my own portrait was done in the style of an Andy Warhol painting, Alternatively, inverting the colour can produce a dramatic effect.*

▶ *Review the colour definitions in the glossary on page 126.*

For every colour surface technique introduced later in the book, there will be more mixing exercises as we try out different techniques with different themes. Remember that this is just an introduction. There is a wealth of art books (see page 127), any of which could be a useful addition to your library of colour and painting techniques.

Remember that colour choices in the world of art also reflect a personal palette. We all have favourite colours, sometimes based on a theme we are presently exploring, or because we just like them. The choices you make are unique to you. Sometimes, the perfect colour is hard to achieve with mixing and you may just have to buy it instead.

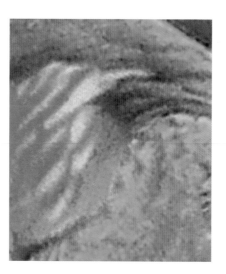

Left: An abstract detail of a parakeet worked in wash. Above: The same area enhanced using an oil-paint filter in Photoshop.

Left, from top to bottom: Photoshop fun – a colour portrait with a posterizing filter; Complementary colours in nature: red and green and blue and orange; Talking parakeets in primary colours; Rocks with the subtlety of greys and soft, neutral colours.

Above and left (detail): **Lightstrike**
(Janet Twinn, UK). Dynamic colour, pattern and
movement with hand-painted and dyed fabric.

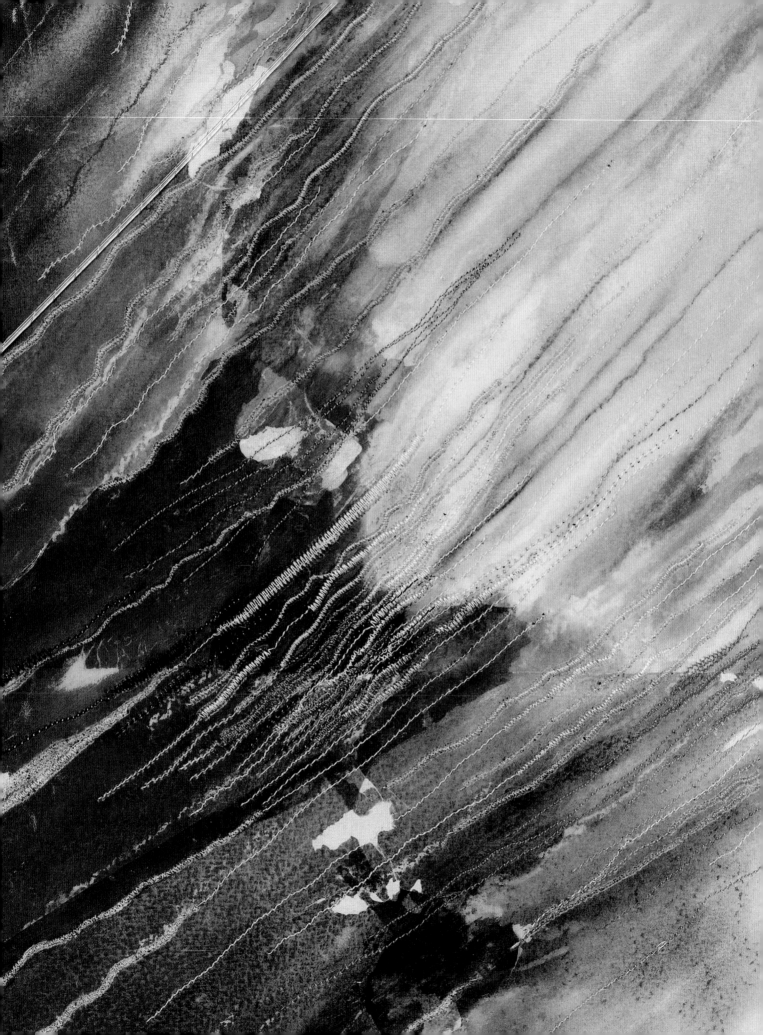

PAINTING

This chapter will include a wide variety of media – from transparent watercolour to thick palette-knife approaches in acrylic – and will provide a good introduction to painting that could inspire textiles. Techniques have been chosen to relate to fabric and stitch, constantly re-enforcing this important connection. Always remember, as you are trying a new material for the first time or revisiting a medium again as a textile artist, to ask yourself how you could achieve the same feeling or essence in fabric. Review your personal list of stitch and surface techniques as you work through the exercises. Art exercises don't always need to be finished in stitch, but continually remind yourself of the possibilities there might be in stitched textiles.

Start with watercolour, followed by gouache, Brusho (Procion dyes work in the same way) and acrylic. It isn't necessary to purchase all the materials at once. The exercises in this chapter can be adapted to any medium; each will create different results. Constant practice is crucial to gaining confidence in painting skills – and you will shortly begin to notice the improvement in your own quilts and textiles.

Continue to look at 'artistic' filter effects from Photoshop Elements or Paint Shop Pro on your reference photos. It's a different way of addressing watercolour, sketch, or acrylic techniques. The results can look flat and computer-generated, but nevertheless they could suggest possibilities when exploring a new subject or personal theme.

Above: **Iceland Sketchbook** (Sandra Meech, UK). Brusho wash and collage.

Left: **Galeforce** (Linda Gleave, UK) This dramatic piece shows the power of the elements.

	Watercolour	Gouache	Brusho	Acrylic	Oil
Basic Selection	Cadmium red, alizarin crimson, lemon and cadmium yellow, yellow ochre, burnt sienna, burnt umber, viridian green, cobalt blue, cerulean blue, phthalo blue and Payne's grey.	Permanent white, process yellow, brilliant red, magenta, process green, process cyan, brilliant blue, violet, burnt umber, neutral grey and lamp black.	Individual pots or in sets; useful colours include lemon, yellow, scarlet, orange, crimson, dark brown, leaf green, turquoise, cobalt blue, black and white. Koh-i-Noor produce watercolour dyes similar to Brusho in a portable travel set.	Titanium white, cadmium red, alizarin crimson, cadmium yellow (lemon) cadmium yellow deep, yellow ochre, ultramarine, phthalo blue, purple, phthalo green, raw umber, burnt sienna, and Payne's grey.	Titanium white, cadmium yellow, lemon yellow, cadmium red, alizarin crimson, ultramarine, cerulean blue, yellow ochre, raw sienna, raw umber, viridian green, Winsor violet, Payne's grey and lamp black. Water-soluble oil-style paints are also available.
Surfaces	Cartridge paper, sized for wet media, and special watercolour paper that has a rougher 'tooth' that resists the drag of the brush - individual sheets or pads. Prepared flat canvases are also available.	Cartridge paper, sized for wet media, in pads or individual sheets and some smooth watercolour papers.	Cartridge paper, sized for wet media, in pads or sketchbooks with at least 110 gsm paper weight. Also works well on black-and-white photocopies for collage.	Prepared paper/card in pads is available with rough and smooth surfaces. Box and prepared canvases can be bought or canvas (calico or linen) stretched over a wood frame and sized with gesso. Hardboard or Masonite, free from grease and with a slight rough surface, will take a layer of primer before painting.	The surfaces for acrylic apply to oil – thick oil paper pads and prepared or stretched canvases. Prepared hardboard or Masonite will also work well.
Brushes	For watercolour, soft brushes are usually used. Begin with a student-priced set. Shape is important – round brushes carry more paint for broad areas, while fan-shaped brushes are useful for blending colour.	Soft brushes as for watercolour – flat brushes for an even area and long and thin ones for fine lines.	A range of soft watercolour-style brushes are useful; use ⅜ or ½in household paint brushes for larger surfaces and sketchbook pages.	Soft bristle brushes (nylon and sable) and hard bristle ('hog' or acrylic) for thick paint. For wash effects use watercolour brushes. Must be cleaned thoroughly immediately after use. Acrylic dries quickly. Palette knives are used for texture.	Oil painting brushes are usually a hard bristle brush. Clean with turpentine or white spirit immediately after use.
Fabrics	On fabric, for a watercolour effect use watered-down fabric paints or Deka silk-style paints and then heat set them. Disperse transfer dyes will also give the same effects on fabrics with a polyester content.	Use directly on cotton but do not wash. A fabric medium could extend the use of gouache on cotton.	Painted on cotton, it will give strong wash effects, but is not permanent and can fade in light.	On fabric there are many varied effects of acrylic on cotton (see page 94). Acrylic inks can be diluted for surface effects. Acrylic can also be used for monoprints and stamp effects on cotton.	Linen, thin canvas or cotton duck can be treated and sized with gesso and other media to take oil paint. Many of the effects are similar to acrylic, but oils do not dry quickly.
Pros & Cons	✓ An essential medium for sketchbooks and travel. Works well with line, tone and mixed media; effects similar to transfer dyes or hand-dyed fabric and the layering of sheers.	✓ Perfect for illustrations or sketchbook observation; more opaque for strong flat colour and shapes.	✓ Inexpensive, safe, non-toxic dye powder paint – gem-like colours that take bleach or wax resists. Used for sketchbook pages and black-and-white photocopies.	✓ Water-soluble, versatile, relatively inexpensive medium, useful for a wide variety of surface effects. Dries quickly, but extender gels can keep paint wet longer.	✓ A favourite medium for fine artists. Very slow drying, so brushwork can be reworked easily. ✗ Not as versatile with fabric and stitch.

Additional general art materials

Watercolour pencils such as Inktense by Derwent (dyes in pencil form).
Masking fluid or a white candle for resists.
Kitchen towel, Clingfilm (Saran Wrap), sponge, dishwashing cloth, cotton buds for smudging.
Chinagraph marker (white and black).
Palettes Plastic palettes for watercolour, gouache and acrylic, or use an old white plate. Acrylic 'staywet' trays or tear-off sheets as pads work well. A wooden palette is used for oils.
Retarding mediums for acrylics will keep paint wet. Gel mediums help increase transparency, matt mediums protect finished work, and modelling pastes and texture gels are used for dimension. For oils, linseed oil will increase the drying time.

Materials for fabrics
Silk paints work on both cotton or silk.
Acrylic paints can be diluted for wash effects.
Freezer paper This silicone-backed paper is ironed on fabric to stabilize it before painting.

Extra 100% cotton fabric for painting and general experiments.
Sheers and organzas for layering, polyester sheers for transfer dyeing.
Disperse transfer dyes for transparent colour effects on cloth (see page 76).
Bondaweb (Wonder Under).
Iron and ironing surface.
Markmaking sticks such as Markal Paintstiks or permanent pens for drawing on cloth.
Bleach pen, or discharge paste used with dyed or discharge black fabric.
Sewing kit, to include stranded cottons and could include a selection of dyed or batik style fabrics.
Sewing machine with a darning foot for free machine embroidery.
Thin wadding (batting) – needlepunch, interfacings, needlepunch or felt for small samples.
Sketchbook, A5 or A4 landscape-shaped, perfect- or spiral-bound or spiral with quality cartridge paper, sized for wet media (but any size will do).

Above: A 'staywet' tray for acrylics.
Below: An assortment of mixed fabrics and threads to dip into.

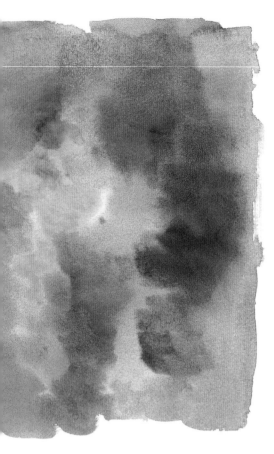

Watercolour

Watercolour is a favourite medium among artists for landscape, detail in nature and still-life subjects. The brightness and fluidity of watercolour makes it popular for water, reflections and sky. It is also a very portable medium for painted sketches of people and of daily life.

Work quickly. The control of this medium can be a challenge, but the freshness and energy on the page is worth the effort. Layers of colour and detail can be added, but it is difficult to erase a mistake, so a few techniques are worth learning from the start. This is a basic introduction to watercolour and there are many more techniques you can discover later. Watercolour artists work at their craft for many years – it doesn't happen overnight.

Basic techniques

Before you start, it might be worth revisiting the chapter on colour to remind you of the numerous mixes that can be achieved. Practise with a few combinations. Consider the transparent qualities created when you over-paint. Watercolours dry lighter than other media and it may be difficult to judge this at first, but you can repeat the overlays to build up colour.

It might be a good idea to have some landscape or still-life reference for inspiration – keep it simple and, although this is only creative 'play', remember composition and centres of interest when choosing an area. As you are exploring the potential of watercolour, continue to consider how this medium could eventually be interpreted in fabric and stitch.

Most of these techniques could also be adapted to gouache and Brusho.

Creating washes

▶ *Dampen your paper with a sponge on all or part of the area and, beginning at the top of the page with a thick square brush, let the colour blend down the page for an overall flat wash. This is good for backgrounds (tip: mix more paint for the background wash than you think you will use).*

▶ *Try some graded washes for distant landscape effects; try these techniques on dry paper as well, for different results. Practise softening the edges with a cotton bud.*

▶ *With landscape in mind, consider contrasts in the intensity of colour, such as using a light wash for sky and clouds, contrasted by dark, distant hills. Clouds can be created by adding extra water to lighten the area, by sponging off some colour or by adding Chinese white or white gouache to the surface.*

▶ *For an abstract approach, just play with wet-on-wet colour to see how the brushstrokes bleed into each other.*

Hint
Have a board to which watercolour paper can be taped; it will keep your work in place and you can apply watercolour washes at a slight angle.

Above, top: Blended washes for fun.
Above: Graded washes for landscape.
Right: A selection of brushes.

Above: This image started with a graded monochromatic wash, then detail of trees was added on top. Below: A splatter-effect colour wash with a pen-and-ink sketch on top.

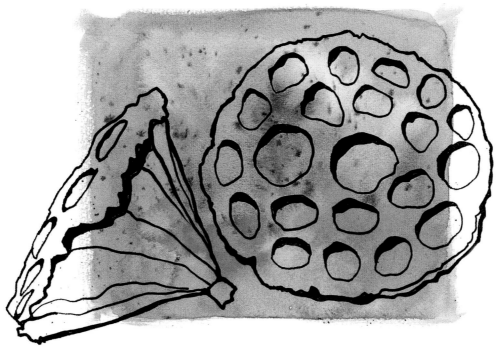

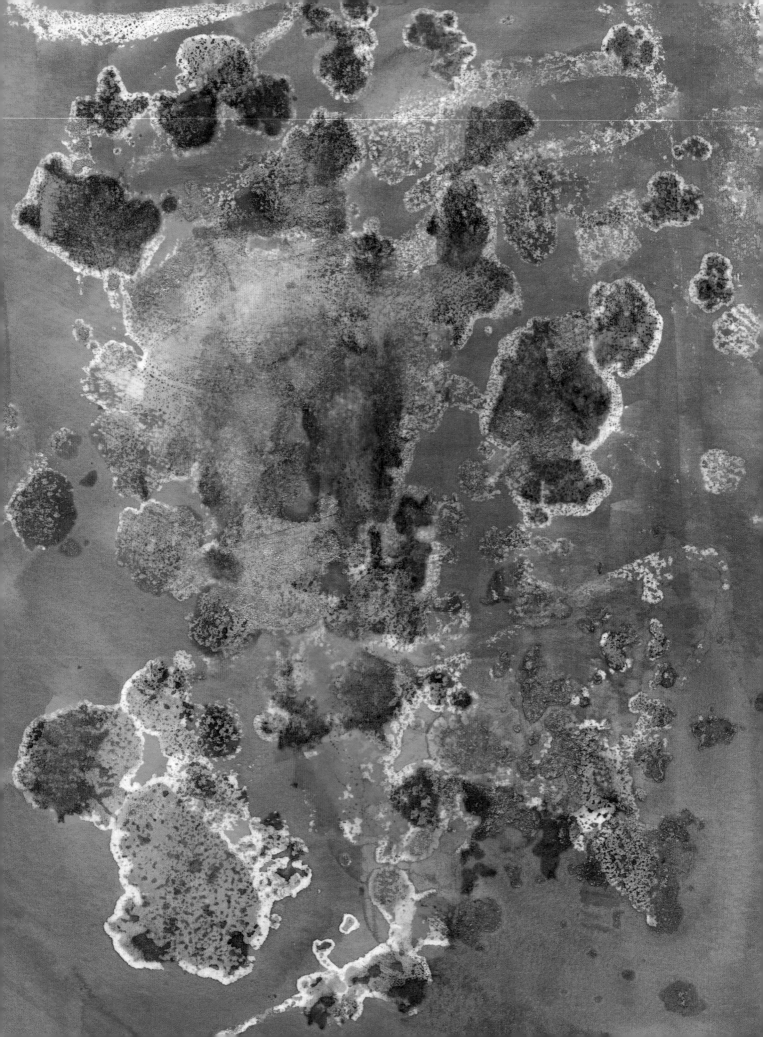

Brush effects

▶ *A large round brush holds more paint and allows for a variety of shapes, creating broad strokes as well as delicate points as thick and thin bands of colour are layered.*

▶ *Splattering, made with a squared brush (cut with a craft knife) or an old toothbrush, produces fine dots of colour on the surface. Low-tack masking tape or paper can be used to isolate certain areas from the splatter effect.*

▶ *Dry-brush techniques could mimic stitch lines or you might consider drawing with a stick for some interesting line detail.*

▶ *White gouache with a fine brush can enhance a highlight.*

Resists and white highlights

▶ *Leaving some areas white will keep a composition vibrant. A light pencil sketch can be used to isolate the area.*

▶ *Masking fluid, applied with a small brush (this must be washed out of the brush immediately after use), acts as a resist with washes and is effective for water or any delicate shapes, such as flowers in a meadow.*

▶ *Highlights can be added with white gouache or a chinagraph marker.*

▶ *Using oil pastels or chinagraph markers for resist drawing can give interesting results.*

Impressing and sponge effects

Clingfilm (Saran Wrap) or a coarse linen or hessian will give interesting effects. If you are using clingfilm, paint the surface and then lay scrunched film on top. When this is removed an interesting marbled pattern will be seen. This technique can also be effective on fabric as well. Bubble wrap and aluminium foil can also be used to impress paint onto a surface.

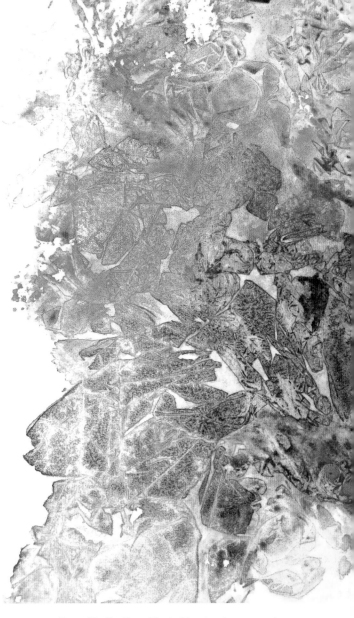

Above: Clingfilm (Saran Wrap) with watercolour or gouache reveals wonderful effects on paper.

Left: Bush walk sketchbook spread, in watercolour. White areas create a more lively composition.

Mallee gum.

Bush walk. near Beaulah Camp.

Left: Wax-crayon scrapings were melted (with parchment and an iron) on paper and painted with watercolour or Brusho.

Above: Watercolour vase with dynamic sections.

Above: White candle resist marks on the paper,
then scrunched and painted with transfer dyes.

Exercises

▸ *Adapt one of your quick one-minute landscape sketches into a small watercolour painting. Keep it small, for easier control, and don't forget to use highlighting tools (chinagraph pencil or gouache).*

▸ *Take a simple still life – perhaps flowers in a vase – and draw it in pencil on watercolour paper. Next, impose a patchwork pattern of lines across the whole surface. Consider each section separately in a watercolour wash, paying attention to light and shade. Highlight as necessary. This exercise could be done with any subject in nature, or with collectibles, architecture or landscape subjects.*

▸ *Collate photos with water or glass reflections for reference. Water is a favourite subject with landscape artists, and beaches and shorelines are popular in textiles. Consider modern architecture and glass and try some effects with watercolour washes.*

▸ *With random colours, create a background, using wet-on-wet merged colour. Find a subject sympathetic to the colours and draw with a black pen on the dried surface. See pages 72 and 73.*

WATERCOLOUR EFFECTS ON FABRIC

Disperse transfer dyes

Disperse transfer dyes can create wonderful watercolour and resist effects on cloth. The colour is permanent when ironed with a hot, dry iron and often more than two or three prints can be achieved.

Paint wash effects on thin layout paper, no larger than A4 or letterhead size (8½ × 11 in), with disperse transfer dyes. A substitute for thin layout paper could be 80gsm copier paper. When dry, the paper is ironed face down onto white or cream fabrics with a high polyester content (polycotton, Vilene [Pellon] interfacings, sateen, linings, curtain lace or polyester organza). Note that some pure cotton fabric that has a tight weave and has been sized (do not wash before use) will also work well with these dyes.

▸ *Resist marks can first be added to the paper with white candle or oil pastel.*

▸ *Scrunch the paper before you paint it – this will give the end result a marbled appearance.*

▸ *Blend colours occasionally and let papers fully dry before transferring the image onto cloth.*

▸ *The dyed paper can be used two or three times if the original dye mix is strong. If disperse transfer dyes are in powder form, use 1tsp to 50ml (2 fl oz) of water and remember that the colours painted on paper will be brighter when transferred.*

▸ *Fabric crayons can be used to make additional marks on the used dye papers for interesting effects.*

▸ *The used paper can be used in mixed-media collage pieces, as it takes stitch well.*

Above left: Clouds and big skies are a favourite subject for watercolour. Above: Wet-on-wet exercise with an autumn landscape in mind. Left: Poppy field in watercolour with a mix of oil pastel and coloured pencil added for detail.

Right: **Evening Glow** (Freda Surgenor, Australia) Fading light and reflections in watercolour.

Hint
Copying black-and-white photocopies with tracing paper at the window or a light box could be a useful technique, but it's always better to practise freehand drawing, and remember that any of these exercises could be incorporated into a sketchbook.

Above: **Blue Door** (Sandra Meech, UK). Beach huts at dusk
in transfer-dyed fabrics, with paper and stitch.

Effects on fabric

▶ *On a smooth polyester sateen, create a drawing with permanent pen. This could also include some writing – perhaps a description or thoughts about the theme. Next, transfer-dye colour onto the surface, ready for stitching.*

▶ *Create a small composition with transferred fabric (copied three times for different intensities), and incorporate the used transfer paper for a small mixed-media piece. Perhaps a contrasting colour of stitch might liven it up?*

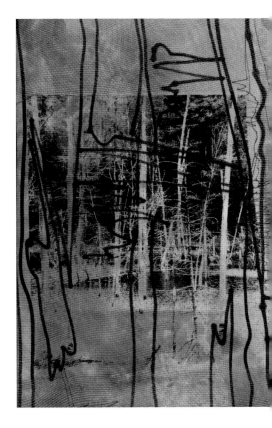

Above: **Autumn** (Sandra Meech, UK). Permanent pen on transfer-dyed sateen, photo imagery and stitch.
Left: **Woodland Walk** (Sandra Meech, UK). Mixed media with transfer dyes. Below: Sketch on sateen with transfer dyes.

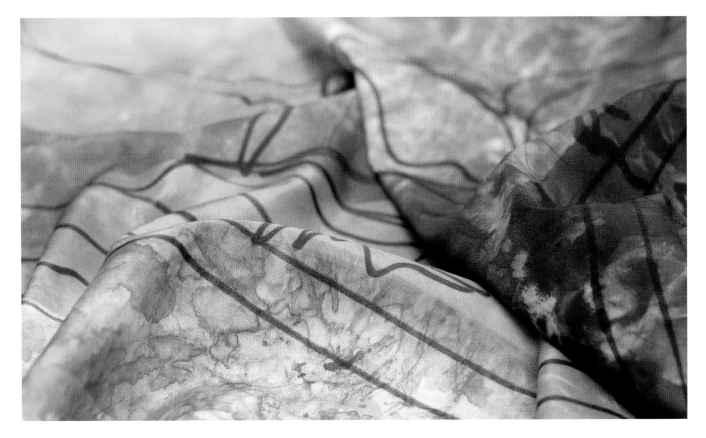

79

Opposite page: **St Pauls, London** (Sandra Meech, UK). Sketch with permanent pen on polyester sateen with transfer dyes, paper and stitch.
Above: **Red Sky at Night** (Sandra Meech, UK). Transfer dyes with transfer paper added.
Left and below (detail): **Rockies Sunset** (Sandra Meech, UK). Intuitive approaches to stitch work well with transfer-dyed compositions.

Above: Isolated section of a photograph done in gouache.

Above: Colourful wools and threads, rendered in an 'artistic' oil-paint filter in Photoshop.

Gouache

One of my favourite media, gouache gives a more substantial, flatter colour that is opaque in nature and is ideally suited for illustration, pattern or design work – and so is great for sketchbooks. The paint dries darker than it looks when wet. It's a good idea to use an old white plate as a palette for mixing colours. The dry colour is easily activated with water, so many watercolour techniques also apply to gouache. When diluted with water, gouache is quite transparent, but if you use it straight from the tube the colour is strong and you can re-work an area. Gouache is a good medium for learning about colour mixing and may work on fabric surfaces more easily than watercolour.

Mixing gouache

▶ *Try the watercolour mixing exercises but remember that gouache is more opaque in appearance. Resists and masking fluid and materials work well, as do oil pastel or candle resists, when combined with a gouache wash.*

Exercises

▶ *Inspiration could come from a small assortment of collectibles, bric-a-brac, junk jewellery, gardening tools or pottery or samples of world textiles – photographed or from life. On smooth cartridge or in your sketchbook, compose an interesting but not too complicated composition, drawing it in pencil first. Begin with a flat pale colour first, and then build and blend colours, paying attention to highlights and shadows. Keep the background simple.*

▶ *Extend a photograph –take half of a favourite photograph and, working freehand, draw the missing part with pencil. Extend the colour to match the photograph as closely as possible.*

▶ *Take inspiration from a city street or an avenue of interesting colourful houses – paying attention to perspective, but keeping it simple, with simple shapes and flat colours. Consider whether to use full colour or a monochrome and the effects of light and shade.*

▶ *Using a portrait as a starting point, consider using a Photoshop Elements filter as a starting point for a gouache painting (see page 66). Remember, any of these exercises could be adapted to fabric with appliqué, image transfer and stitch.*

Right: Black-and-white image of beach huts painted with dilute gouache.

Using fabric

Many of the art exercises suggested above could be developed into a stitched textile.

► *Isolate a section of a finished painting or sketch. Use hand-dyed fabrics or Bali/batik-style ones to amass a supply of bright or subtle colours. Iron Bondaweb (Wonder Under) to the back of each fabric and cut out small shapes that look like brushstrokes. Iron these onto a neutral background (use baking parchment or Teflon sheet) to create a small fabric painting. Stitch it by machine and then add hand 'marks' for interest. Consider starting with a small sample, but note that this technique can be adapted to any size, including a pieced or appliquéd quilt.*
► *Transfer any small painting (gouache or watercolour) onto cloth, using a simple heat-transfer method (see page 111) as a background for machine and hand stitching.*

Remember that by further 'windowing' or isolating an area of your work you continue to abstract the design.

Above: Sketchbook spread of
Australian bush plant.

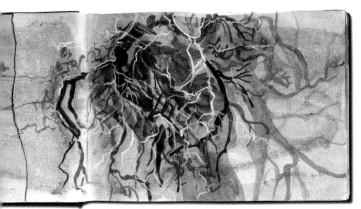  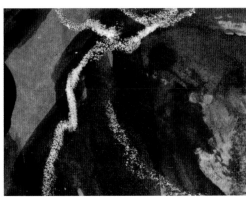

Above left: Detail of a sketch heat-transferred
onto cotton ready for stitch. Middle and right:
Abstract sections for further textile inspiration.
Left: Flowering rock plants in Iceland, painted
in gouache with oil-pastel highlights.

Art Class 7
Wet media still life

There are several approaches to this class, which was inspired by a photo of dramatic flowers (1). The flowers were first sketched on cartridge with ink (2), using a calligraphy pen (any black mark-making tool will work). The line drawing is then photocopied for reference. Oil or chalk pastels are added as colour is built up (3). Alternatively, you might use Neocolour (water-soluble oil pastel sticks) for an extra wash. Don't forget to try a sketch in coloured pencil (4).

Blocks of colour in a flat wash are placed where the flowers are positioned (6). The black-line photocopy is printed onto acetate, which can be laid over many different backgrounds to create various effects.

On fabric, the background for the still life can be painted with wash and the line drawing interpreted in a stitched line. Couching thicker thread or wool could create a very strong surface design.

1. **Rudbeckia at Waterperry**; 2. Pen-and-ink line drawing; 3. Chalk pastel on line drawing; 4. Coloured pencil sketch; 5. Quick watercolour painting; 6. Blocks of colour in gouache with line; 7. Abstract section of the same image.

Brusho

Brusho dyes are similar to Procion, but are used for colouring paper. Brusho is a powder that is mixed with water and creates luscious and intense colours and, as it is a dye, the colour can be discharged with bleach. Useful for preparing sketchbook pages for use, Brusho colours can be mixed and applied to larger surfaces. Brusho is only designed to be used on paper and, although it acts like a dye in that resists work well and colour can be bleached out, it can fade with light.

▶ *Black-and-white photocopies, newspaper, magazine paper or white cartridge paper can be painted with Brusho. Resist marks could be made first with white-candle resist, and shapes could have been stamped with masking fluid, or oil pastes used for movement and pattern. The coloured papers can be used on their own for collage or scanned into the computer and transferred onto fabric for a stitched piece.*

Right: Black-and-white photocopy with candle resist reflects Canadian woodlands ravaged by the pine beetle.

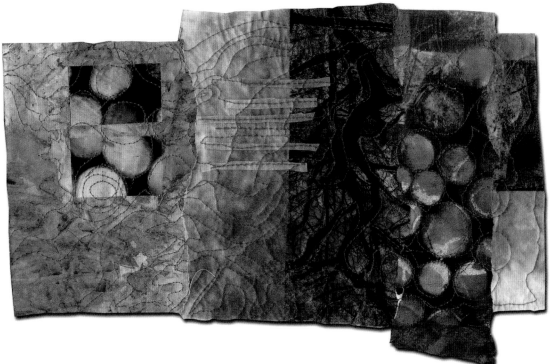

Left: **Woodland** (Sandra Meech, UK). Mixed media, painted papers, transfer-dyed fabrics and stitch.

en route to Mildura on the bus.

Above: Travelling to Mungo. In this sketchbook study, movement is created with coloured pencil and oil pastel.

Creating a sketchbook

If you make a habit of using your sketchbook regularly, this will help you to gain confidence with art skills as observation and detail is explored for future reference. If you work this way for several months, you will consolidate your ideas as your sketchbook becomes a record of your own personal 'journey' – a private place for ideas, written words and thoughts.

Sketchbooks can serve very different purposes, ranging from an important personal record of sketches and ideas to visual journals and diaries, embellished mixed-media journals or altered books. Remember that some decorative book styles never include real ideas for future development into stitched textiles. Book construction is, however, an art form in itself, and 3-D bound and stitched books can be creative and clever in their own right.

We often have the privilege to see notations and sketches in the sketchbooks of the 'great masters', including intimate studies or observations of the human anatomy. Consider Leonardo da Vinci's scientific ideas and drawings, which were centuries ahead of his time. Displayed artists' sketchbooks can also reveal either an intense or playful record of the individual's life – personal observations never meant for viewing, but nevertheless marvellous to see.

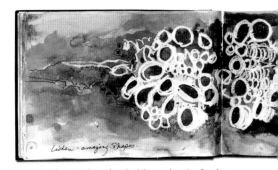

Above: Lichen sketch. Oil-pastel resist, Brusho and line.

Preparation

Sketchbooks vary in size and structure – popular types including the spiral-bound landscape format as well as perfect-bound varieties. The spiral A5 landscape size is good for sketching 'in situ', as the hard cover is folded back to rest between elbow and wrist. Otherwise, any good-quality sketchbook is worth the investment. Cartridge paper should be at least 120 to 140 gsm in weight, acid free and preferably sized to take washes. Cartridge is a fine surface and takes pencil, oil pastels, pens and resists with wax and bleach.

The whole experience of painting white pages first is very liberating. Perhaps you could use your sketchbook to explore a variety of different themes, working through subjects such as landscape, still life, detail in nature, architecture or simple figures from life. Another sketchbook might involve a more specific theme and colour selection, with thoughts and ideas directly relating to a future textile series.

Left: **Dorset (detail)** (Sandra Meech, UK). Transferred imagery with stitch. This textile piece shows trees wasted by the pine beetle.

Above: Sketchbooks, including altered, collage-covered, and Japanese stab-bound varieties.

Consider the following ideas:

▶ *Painting a series of full-page spreads (the left- and right-hand pages as one) with two colours (each spread can be different) painted diagonally across the whole surface. Work quickly, turning wet pages over and continuing. The monoprint effects achieved in this way are wonderful and a work of art on their own. Specific washes are ideal for certain uses:*

a) Medium to dark colour combinations, for drawings with dark shadows with added light highlights.

b) A dilute wash over several spreads, for drawings in line and colour and writing.

c) Landscape-style wash, for big skies or high horizons at one-third and two-thirds proportions; vary the colour for dark and brooding or light and bright effects.

d) Spreads left blank for quick sketches and detail drawings and painting, for diary writings, notes, observation or a collage of photo references.

▶ *Resists – oil pastel (white or light colours) or a white candle will create interesting marks, as several pages will be affected.*

▶ *On completion, bring the front and back covers together and spread out the pages in a circular fan to dry overnight. The pages will crinkle but will eventually flatten when the book is closed.*

Above top: Sketchbook detail from a peeling and rusted wall. Oil pastel and wash.
Above middle: Collage images with added wash in gouache. Above: This sketchbook page has been scratched to resemble an ice floe.
Right: The above image adapted to an ice lagoon photo, transferred and ready for stitch.

88

Right: An assortment of
sketching materials, oil
pastels and coloured
pencils.

Left: Pathways 1 and 2. Sketchbook spreads,
collage of images, painting and writings that
inspired the final textile piece shown below.

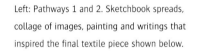

Left: **Pathways** (Sandra Meech, UK). Over 3.5m
(11¹⁄₂ft) long, this piece represents a woodland
journey, using imagery, transfer-dyed sateen
and machine stitch.

Left: Fabric prepared using permanent pen
with transfer dyes on sateen.

89

Art Class 8
Reflections and stitch

Reflections on water are a wonderful inspiration for textiles. This realistic approach can become abstract when detail is enlarged. For these exercises, use gouache and isolate an interesting section from a photograph. The photograph could be enlarged in black and white to help reference the pencil drawing as you draw on cartridge paper.

- It may seem like a 'paint by numbers' type of approach, but the difference is that you will be choosing the design and the colours. Don't forget to blend any colours, as necessary.

- This painting will be perfect translated into fabric. Consider a size of 20 x 50cm (8 x 20in), for a long and thin composition. On a small scale, bonded and machine stitched appliqué methods might be best, but if your design is taken much larger it could be pieced. Cut-back or reverse appliqué methods could also work, with the defining satin stitch between colours.

- Everyone is fascinated by the glass reflections on modern buildings, as each pane of glass is often slightly different from the next and therefore unique. Find or take photographs, looking at the building 'head on'. Consider each section and enjoy the movement and distortion. Try capturing this in several small line drawings first, and then adapt your sketches to gouache, considering the shapes, how the sky changes colour and the curved lines. Perhaps one of these line drawings could be taken further, to create a small wall hanging with curved seams and machine quilting.

Top: Reykjavik harbour boats photograph. Above: A section from the photograph was isolated and painted in gouache. The next step in the process could be raw-edge appliqué with machine and hand stitch.

Opposite page: **South Bank Reflection** (Sandra Meech, UK). Photo imagery with painted fabric and stitch. Left: This modern layered-glass sculpture provided inspiration for the piece.

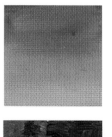

Acrylics

Acrylic paint is water-soluble, but the pigment is bound with a synthetic acrylic medium which dries to a thin film of colour. These paints, which were developed in the 1950s, are quick-drying and waterproof, making them a very versatile medium. They can be used in transparent washes or as an impasto (thick, textured brushstroke), for texture. Manufacturers have developed additives to retard the drying time, which permits a more controlled blending of colour, compared with oils. Acrylics come in tubes or in bottles, in the form of acrylic inks. They can be painted onto most surfaces without any advanced preparation, so they can work well with textile applications.

Basic techniques

The following ideas suggest a few simple ways of using acrylic paint, but there are many more techniques that might be worth exploring (see page 127 for further reading).

Try colour-combination exercises first as these are always an important first step.

Paint directly from the tube
- *Brush on an even, flat colour.*
- *For impasto techniques, use thicker paint, applied with two or three other colours – blend colours together first, then dab on broken colour.*
- *'Scumbling' is when wet paint is added to a dry, textured layer of paint.*
- *A palette knife can be used to apply pigment in broad strokes.*

Textured media
- *Using a knife, mix acrylic with sand.*
- *Mix it with other commercial texture gels and mediums.*
- *Using a mix of acrylic and some other medium, try effects with clingfilm (Saran Wrap).*
- *Apply a thick spread and then scrape back with a fork or other toothed tools (those found for plaster effects).*

Wash effects
- *Work in watercolour with thin washes made by just adding water. Try a graded wash.*
- *Add a thicker version of the same colour from the tube, with a little white added – the colour will be strong, but have a feeling of gouache.*
- *Use a glaze with a thin amount of colour, for transparent effects.*

Top: A selection of acrylic techniques to try, including wash and blended colour, impasto and flat colour, scumbling and palette-knife techniques, dry-brush and sgraffito effects. Above: Vase detail from page 76 rendered in acrylic wash. Right: A selection of acrylic and gouache paints and brushes.

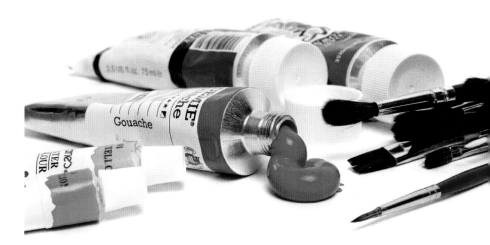

Hint
Many of the previous exercises with watercolour and gouache could be repeated with acrylics, yielding very different results. Remember that acrylics dry quickly, so your brushes need to be washed immediately after use.

Left: **Iceland Revisited** (Sandra Meech, UK). A quick acrylic painting on canvas.
Below: **Iceland Revisted I** (Sandra Meech, UK). As a stitched-textile piece, acrylic on cotton, layered and stitched.

Above: Tassie stitchbook page – acrylic on fabric with paper collage and additional wash, ready for stitch.

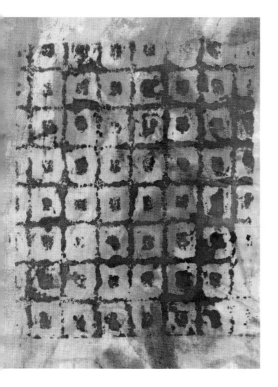

Above: Acrylic-painted cloth with additional stamp from textured vinyl wallpaper (see page 96).

On fabric

Acrylic paint in one form or another has recently become a valuable material for the expressive textile artist. When thick artist's acrylic is painted directly onto cotton, this will considerably stiffen the surface and, if the paint is too thick, it will be impossible to stitch the fabric by machine. If the acrylic is diluted to create a wash, the colour spreads and there is less control. This can create some interesting effects, so it is worth a try. Mixed 50:50 with a fabric medium, the fabric will have a softer surface, so hand stitching is easier. Surfaces will fade slightly in colour if washed, but the effect is very appropriate for wall hung art quilts.

Dry brush A bristle brush can give a soft edge and a broken-colour effect on the surface. Only a small amount of paint is needed on the brush. This method can be used to suggest texture and it's best to start by using it for a simple still-life subject.

Sgraffito The painted surface is scratched or 'scored' to reveal the colour beneath, which could be the white of the canvas or another layer of colour. Layers are added and lines are scratched back to reveal line detail and texture. Try letting the layer begin to dry before scraping back with a sharp knife (scalpel) or paint knife, or with a blunter implement (for a less defined line).

Texturing the surface This can be great fun – acrylic modelling paste, applied with a palette knife or comb, will give wonderful pattern and texture. Imprints from bubble wrap, clingfilm (Saran Wrap) or something similar could be added. Perhaps adding string or open-weave hessian could be interesting. When this has dried, apply paint in thin glazes, which can be dabbed on and rubbed back for interesting effects. Thicker paint can be added for highlight. Consider using this approach for the collagraphs on page 124.

Mixing different media with acrylic

A pencil sketch is transformed with opaque acrylic washes – finished with coloured pencils, for definition. Try this with a simple landscape, a detail in nature or a still life from your favourite photographs.

Pastels can be used in a similar way, being layered and blended to give movement and texture to the surface.

Charcoal, when added to acrylic, will give added depth and character to the subject. Perhaps this would work well with a detail from a selection of world textiles. The blending of charcoal is useful for adding light and shade.

Paper and acrylic, in the form of a mixed-media collage, is another way to extend this wonderful medium. This can be a valuable addition to sketchbooks and is a major contribution to the changed typed page in an altered book. The acrylic allows some background information to come through, but provides another surface for additional media – drawing, sketching, painting and even stitching.

Pointillist brushstrokes can also be effective. Look at a small section of an Impressionist painting for inspiration. This could work with gouache paint as well.

Hint

Always stabilize cotton by ironing it onto freezer paper (a silicone-sided paper, used to prevent condensation in foods for the freezer).

Above: **Northwest Passage** (Sandra Meech, UK). Palette-knife painting in acrylic transferred onto cotton ready for stitch.

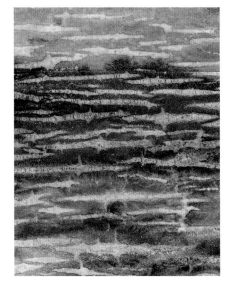

Top: Dilute acrylic on Bondaweb could inspire a landscape piece. Above: Scrunched dilute acrylic on Bondaweb creates an organic effect.

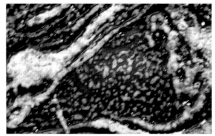

Above: Acrylic painted onto textured vinyl wallpaper then printed off onto cotton.

Consider experimenting with the effects suggested below.

▶ *Palette-knife paintings on cloth with acrylic and fabric medium could create a fabric to be incorporated into a landscape or cityscape textile composition. You could also try this on different fabrics, including sheers and coloured or hand-dyed surfaces.*

▶ *Acrylic paint on Bondaweb (Wonder Under) or Vilene (Pellon) can give a variety of effects.*
a) Paint a very thin watery acrylic liquid onto the glue (rough) side of the surface. Work with the grain of the Bondaweb, which is at right angles to the curled edge. Apply watered-down paint very quickly; soon, the glue begins to shrink, creating a wonderful linear appearance. When dry (after 24 hours), iron face down onto cotton. This can be incorporated into any textile composition, but cannot be re-ironed.
b) Paint a watery layer of acrylic over the Bondaweb, then quickly lift and manipulate the glue on the paper. Leave to dry for 24 hours, then iron off onto cotton. Wonderful transparent organic shapes could remind us of stone, reflections or water – indeed, any surface, either natural or urban.

▶ *Acrylics (try pearlized, metallic paints or iridescent gels) can be lightly brushed or rubbed onto a heavily quilted surface to give dimension and texture.*

▶ *Oil pastel and acrylic on cotton – first stabilize the cotton with freezer paper; create a freehand drawing with black or dark oil pastels and heat set with baking parchment. Next, begin to paint with a combination of acrylic and a fabric medium. Peel off the freezer paper; add a thin wadding and backing fabric, and the fabric is ready for stitching. You could try contouring by machine or adding seeding stitch, for shadow effects.*

▶ *Acrylic can be painted on textured vinyl wallpapers to create watery or distressed wall textures. A small section can be used as a stamp on white cotton, then further painted and rubbed back for good results. Layered with some interfacing on the back, it also takes machine stitch very well. Bear in mind that small sections of paper can easily be incorporated into a larger stitched textile.*

▶ *A painting can be scanned, and then heat-transferred onto cloth, with more paint added for fun. Stitching through very thick acrylic paint will break needles, so caution is needed.*

Above: This acrylic sketch of a poppy field was heat-transferred twice – one version for cutting and adding sheers to for a machine-stitch composition and the other for hand stitch.

Left: **Poppy Field I**
(Sandra Meech, UK)
– a psychedelic
version of the
poppy field image
below, using
complementary
colours, has
dynamic,
expressive
potential.
Below left:
Poppy Field
(Sandra Meech, UK)
– a quick acrylic
painting done in
Scotland.

Art Class 9
Into the abstract

A wonderful starting point for an abstract painting is to enlarge and 'window' a favourite photograph several times and then take a section from this. The essence of shape and pattern remains evident, but the composition has been simplified for a more dynamic contemporary approach. Also study the image in black and white to notice more abstract shapes, and don't forget to rotate or mirror the subject for different results. Try several compositions and then choose one.

In fabric you could:
- Paint directly on cotton, adding stitching to define detail
- Use appliqué methods to piece or apply sections of dyed, painted or commercial fabrics – keep the whole thing simple and small to start with.

Remember that small painted and stitched pieces can be presented in a frame or mounted on canvas.

Hint
Fabric paints are often thinner in consistency than artist's acrylics, but they offer another way of colouring cloth and come in a great variety of colours (brand names include Pebeo Setacolour and Deka silk paints, both of which are heat set).

Top: Marlborough vineyard, NZ. Above: The same photo inverted (black to white), angled and cropped for an abstract effect.

Left: **Relics (Uberbleibsel)** (Esther Wagner, Germany). Random transfer-dyed images form a subtle but exciting background for mixed-media collage with stitch.

Above: **Winter Vineyard** (Lura Schwarz Smith, USA). A wonderful use of painted imagery and fabrics in an abstract way.

Oil paints

Oil paints have been used by artists and great masters since the 15th century and are still favoured by fine artists today. When oils are used as washes or as a textured 'impasto' (applied thickly with brush or palette knife), there are some similarities to acrylics, but because of the linseed oil base, oil paints do not dry very quickly, so the artist can work at their own pace, adjusting and re-working the surface more slowly. Oils are mixed and blended in a similar way to acrylics and it's worth taking a little time to experiment.

▶ *Always be thinking about the connection with fibre surfaces and stitch 'marks' as you paint.*

Hint

Oil paints dry very slowly and also have a strong odour, so a ventilated space is essential. They are available in a water-based form for ease of use at beginner level, but it is worth having real artist's oil paints to try.

Basic techniques

Many of the techniques covered in acrylics can also be used for oils (see pages 92–97), but there are some additional things to try...

▶ *Coloured grounds – a thin coloured wash or background can be a great place to start. It adds an underlying vibrancy to a painting. When over-worked with brushstrokes, some patches of the ground are left between brushstrokes, which help to unify the whole composition. This could be tried equally effectively with either a landscape or a still-life composition.*

▶ *Dry brush is worth a try with oils; if you use a fan brush for detail in the foreground, great dimension can be achieved. The fan brush is also a useful tool for leaves and other types of vegetation.*

▶ *A variety of marks – consider trying a small painting that would work with marks that you may have done in the first chapters on pencil or charcoal; the different shapes will give energy to the piece.*

▶ *Hard and soft edges are a perfect technique for sky and clouds. In any photograph of the sky, you can see a variety of surfaces in clouds. You can blend oils with a brush or with a finger for the soft edges. Thicker paint, finely applied, will be used for the detailed highlights. In a landscape, blurred or softer edges will be in the background, while harder, sharper strokes are in the foreground.*

Left: **Whatever** (Sandra Meech, UK). Brusho, oil paint, pastels on paper and collage.

Right, top and bottom: **Shopping Again** (**detail**) (Jae Maries, UK). Oil on canvas, appliquéd fabric and stitch.

Above: Building reflections in the oil paint-effect filter in Photoshop Elements.

Exercises

Try some of the earlier exercises in the section on acrylics – most will adapt well in oils. In addition, you could consider the exercises suggested below.

▶ *Underdrawing – working from a head-and-shoulders portrait photograph and thinking of proportion (see page 29), create a background drawing with charcoal. After this has been fixed, layers of paint can be applied, slowly. Don't be tempted to fill everything in, but leave some of the drawing to show through.*

▶ *Complementary colours have been used very successfully by artists to produce lively landscapes. If you use the opposite range of colours on the wheel, a very abstract, contemporary approach can be achieved. Consider a detail of a village scene done this way. Even the sky and shadows are different colours.*

▶ *Photoshop Elements – using a favourite photograph, heighten the saturation and change the hue of colour. A small cropped section of the result could become the starting point for an oil or acrylic painting.*

▶ *Another artistic effect to try in Photoshop Elements is to isolate a section of a favourite photograph and use the oil paint filter on it. This might could be a starting point for a painting that could later translate to applied fabric and stitch.*

Working in fabric

For fabric to work with oil paints, you will need to use a substantial cotton, cotton duck, linen or canvas, and it must be treated with a sealant (gesso or similar) first. Oils will not dry as quickly as acrylics. This may have its limitations, but the advantage is that you can still stitch through the surface.

Return to the world of art – isolate a small area of a contemporary painting for inspiration as you create your own painting on cloth. Add fabric in some areas and marks in stitch in vibrant or subtle colours.

Left: **Poppy Field I (detail)** (Sandra Meech, UK). The full piece is shown on page 97.
Right: **Midnight in Akureyri, Iceland** (Sandra Meech, UK). A quick acrylic palette-knife painting evocative of the photographs. Sections could inspire a textile.

Art Class 10
Getting in the Mood

This painting will be an abstract and more evocative interpretation, which could be inspired by any theme, feeling or subject. This will be expressive, liberating and fun. Use a palette knife and scraping tools for 'sgraffito' marks or flat brushes with thicker paint.

Think of a range of colours, including some neutral hues with one or two small amounts of a startling 'extra', for that wow factor. Analogous combinations work well. Consider adding black, for a dark mood, or white, for a light, ethereal feeling, to a range of colours. For example, if the environment was an underwater marine landscape with tropical fish, the colour range could include blues, greens and turquoise for the water, with splashes of orange, red, yellow and purple for the fish and plants. Or perhaps, for a complete contrast, you might interpret a city street after a rain... at night, with reflections, greyness and monochromatic colours, and touches of neon yellow, red and green.

Paintings, like textile art, can be realistic, contemporary, abstract, concept-driven, expressive or driven by mood and emotion. We can move from one style to another freely, work any size we want and explore creative potential that was always there, but is now realised.

Top: A sunset scene in May in Iceland. Above: The same image with the colours 'inverted' for fun.

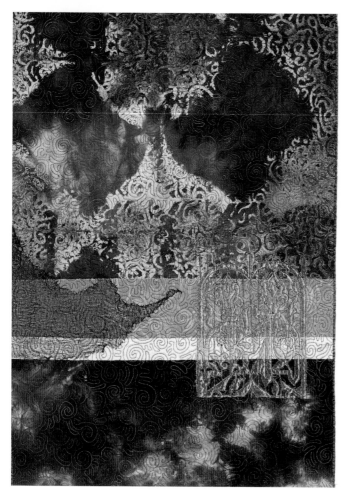

Above: A mixed-media collage used as a starting point for a series (shown above and opposite).

Art Class 11
Working in series

Perhaps a series of small expressive paintings in any medium or mix of your choice, and on any theme, could eventually inspire a series of stitched-textile pieces for the future.

By using a photograph in at least six different ways, we can isolate abstract sections that will become the starting point for several small paintings. This could be on any subject of your choice. Each one becomes a simple painting that could go on to inform a stitched-textile piece. Three or four of these might be finished as a series. Written words can give your painting interest.

Back to basics

Now, with new and different materials explored, the time has come when the vital connection with fabric and stitched textiles becomes more evident. Experimenting with drawing and painting materials though different media on paper, canvas and fabric will hopefully have unleashed hidden talents that were always there, but never nurtured.

This could also have been that vital 'kick start' needed to get going again. These techniques and exercises are timeless, not just another 'must do' workshop or 'must have' sewing material or product, but skills that can be practised for the rest of your life. Continue to review that list of skills you made earlier and see how they directly connect now with the art skills you have acquired. Pin it up as a constant reference every time you put pen or pencil to paper or a brush to the canvas. You may already see the influence of art practice in your stitched textiles, as well as more composed, confident and perhaps better abstract photographs.

Above and above left: **Souvenirs 17–20, Alhambra series** (Charlotte Yde, Denmark).
A wonderful series based on travels and memories.

Above: The same collage broken into different sections that would become a stitched-textile series.

Above: A sketchbook collage that has been manipulated in another colourway in Photoshop for inspiration.

MIXED MEDIA

No review of art techniques would be complete without considering mixed-media approaches. This is one of the closest disciplines to stitched textiles in the 'art world'. Unfairly, 'art' is promoted as being very different to 'craft', and a fine artist who might combine some fabric and mark-making stitches with paint on canvas is considered a 'mixed-media artist'. But, when hung on a wall, an art quilt that is a collage of paint, paper, plastics with fabric and stitch is labelled 'craft'. This will continue to be an issue until quilt and stitched textile artists can have their work taken more seriously and hung in the same 'fine art' galleries as other works of art.

The term 'mixed media' covers a wide spectrum of subjects, from collage, image transfer, monoprinting, screen printing, linocuts and collagraphs to the use of plastics, wire and wood or scrunched, folded or pleated papers and cloth. This section won't cover all possibilities, but it does explore some 2- and 3-dimensional approaches in sketchbooks and for textiles. Collage is one of the most important techniques to master, as it can be inspired by so many subjects and include such a variety of materials.

Left: Machine threads stitched onto soluble material catch the light when mounted 'off the wall'.

Above, left and right (detail): **Middle Earth** (Mandy Ginsberg, Australia). From a wonderful series of embellished stitched-textile work evocative of detail and texture in the landscape.

Collage

Collage means 'rework', from the French word coller ('to stick'), and describes a picture that is made by gluing a number of other elements to it, such as paper, fabric or photographs, combined with paint and other surface textures.

Collage is a medium that is continually transforming and moving into unexplored areas. It offers great opportunities to include imagery on paper, fabrics, embroidery, paint or simple stitching in an expressive and abstract way. Consider Braque, Picasso, Rauschenberg, Paul Klee, Jean Dubuffet or Peter Blake, all of them fine artists who have brought collage and mixed media to the world of art. A collage benefits from a kind of visual language and a unifying theme as colour and texture, light and heavy media or opaque and transparent elements are brought together.

Today, decorative, illustrated journals are popular and often include ephemera – found objects, jewellery and glitz, combined with photo collage. Some might consider these 'art', but the connection is rarely made with this and stitched textiles. Perhaps, with time, this will change and the works of textile artists will be fully appreciated.

Above: **Low tide** (Sandra Meech, UK). Mixed-media stitched collage of fabric, wool and painted papers.
Below: **Arctic Thaw** (Sandra Meech, UK). Gel medium and scrim with embroidery stitch.
Below right: **Inuit Woman I** (Sandra Meech, UK). A mix of painted paper pulp with string, transferred imagery and embroidery stitch.

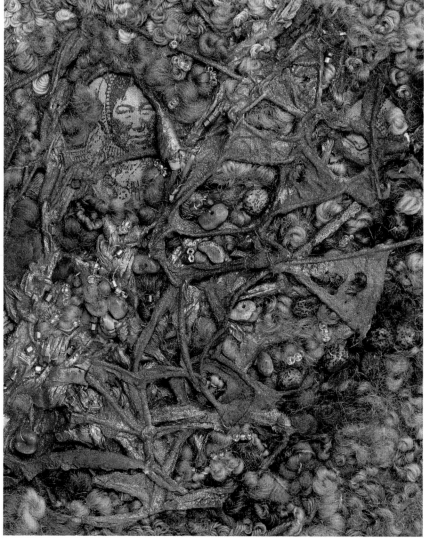

Useful materials to include and equipment

▶ *Interesting papers, handmade textured papers, tissue, newspapers, magazine papers, colour copies (photos on your own theme), black-and-white photocopies, textured vinyl wallpaper, ephemera (bills, tickets, anything that could be part of a personal subject), diary writings.*

▶ *Reference material on a personal theme, such as writings, photos, magazine or newspaper articles; also consider any collected twigs, stones, shells (anything to relate to a theme) – if these are small enough, they could be included; also build a repertoire of shapes, either found or created yourself (leaves, fruit or trees, for example), repeat patterns or stylized motifs and logos – all could be used for inspiration.*

▶ *Gel mediums and texture gels, gesso.*

▶ *Acrylic paints, oil pastels, charcoal with other mark-making tools, an assortment of brushes and a palette knife.*

▶ *Plastics – clingfilm (Saran Wrap), bubble wrap.*

▶ *Fabrics – nets, sheers, natural and synthetic fabrics, hand-dyed fabrics, hessian, scrim, open-weave muslins.*

▶ *String, cord, perhaps small parts from broken implements, watch parts, nails and flat metal bits.*

▶ *Wood glue, PVA glue (it's also useful to have a glue gun).*

▶ *Craft knife and board, other scraping tools.*

▶ *Firm backgrounds for art-based collage could include canvas, hardboard or plywood or, for paper experiments, foamboard.*

▶ *Any other art materials and drawing equipment you might prefer.*

▶ *Baking parchment could be useful.*

Basic techniques

These techniques can be used for collages on a heavy cartridge, foamboard or thicker card stock.

▶ *Tissue paper – apply glue to the surface, add pieces of tissue and manipulate them. When dry, paint the collage with acrylic or metallic paints, for added interest.*

▶ *Waxed pages can be dripped or painted – acrylic or beeswax can be used.*

▶ *Make a collage with Brusho, watercolour or Procion-painted black-and-white photocopies, newsprint or magazines on a personal theme.*

▶ *Oil pastel can be added to printed papers and scratched back.*

▶ *Use dribbled clear PVA, for an abstract pattern, or painted textured vinyl wallpapers, rubbed with acrylic.*

▶ *Gesso and scraped marks can be added; texture gels also work well.*

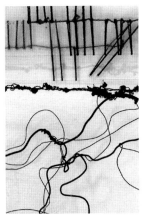

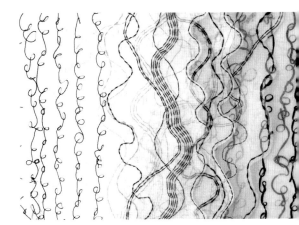

Right top: **3 Rows (detail)** (Amelia Newton, UK). Gesso on canvas with plastic and stitch.
Middle, left: **Significant Things series, Trails (detail)** (Mair Edwards, UK). Black wire.
Middle, right: **Mapping the Valley series, Shadow (detail)** (Mair Edwards, UK). Black wire and thread, plastic. Right: **Rhythm of the Rivers (detail)** (Mair Edwards, UK). Wire and stitch with sheers.

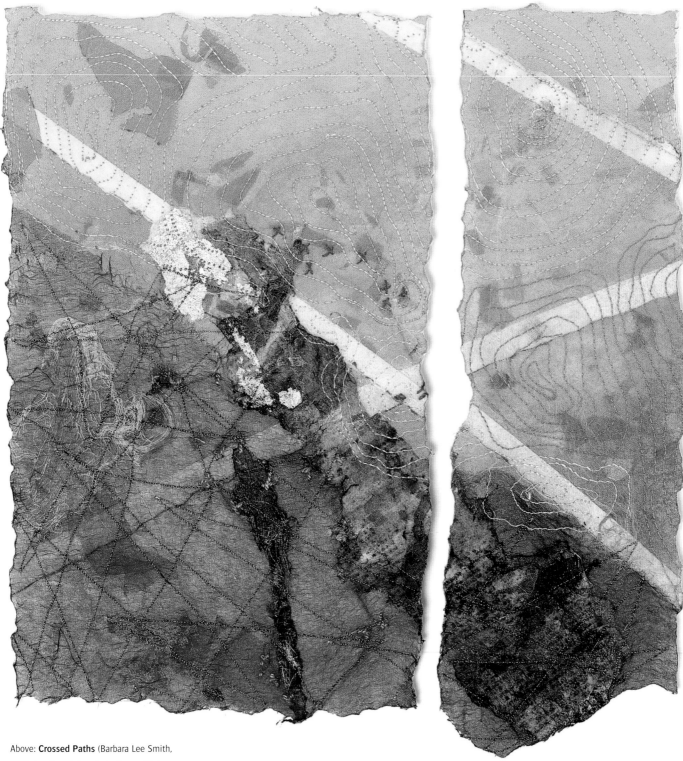

Above: **Crossed Paths** (Barbara Lee Smith, USA). Acrylic paint on Lutradur, applied elements with stitch.

Fabric techniques for use in collage

▶ *PVA-stiffened scrim (bandage muslin) – a small portion of scrim is pulled and manipulated, flattened onto black plastic (liner) and painted with thinned PVA glue (acrylic paint in any colour could be added as well). Once this has dried, the material can be used in mixed-media work.*

▶ *Plastic with acrylic – thin page protectors are cut and opened and slightly thinned acrylic paint is painted on one side. It will seem to resist the acrylic, which is normal.*

Lay the other side down quickly, for a monoprint effect; separate the two sides and leave them to dry thoroughly (24 hours). This can then become a film used to heat-trap fine bits (with the aid of bonding powder and baking parchment) on a colourful cotton surface.

▶ *Any line drawing, coloured painting or sketchbook page that can be scanned into a computer can be heat-transferred onto cloth and then sections of this could be used in a collage.*

▶ *Transfer-dyed or acrylic-painted Lutradur (a non-woven industrial material) can be shaped with a heat tool to create interesting edges or negative spaces.*

▶ *Painted and heat-shrunk Tyvek can also be used for textures.*

▶ *Stamp effects can be made on cloth with vinyl wallpapers or any other stamps you have to hand, using fabric paints or screen inks. Metallics work well and can be stamped onto an already-stitched piece.*

▶ *Screen inks onto cloth, using scraping tools, forks or cut card for pattern.*

▶ *Rubbings can be made on stabilized cotton with oil pastel, and then heat set.*

▶ *Painted acrylic or gesso gives cotton a stiff surface that is perfect for stitch/sketchbook pages.*

▶ *Images transferred onto cloth are an important addition to collage.*

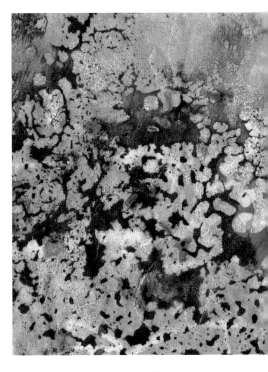

Above: Plastic first painted with acrylic then used for trapping threads in small cut 'bits' for use in mixed-media or stitch collage.

Hint

Do not work on too large a scale. Try a small image – A5 or half of a letterhead-size image. The larger the size, the more difficult it is to apply a hot, even heat over the surface, unless you have a heat press.

Photo image transfer

Image transfer has been mentioned frequently. Not only can this provide photographic real images on cloth for piecing, appliqué or mixed-media collage, but any sketch, drawing, painting or interesting surface can also be captured this way. A finished stitched textile can be recycled, to be included in a fresh new piece. The possibilities are endless. Heat transfer and the use of an acrylic medium are two methods mentioned here in depth. Other techniques include treated and stabilized paper-backed cotton, which can be fed directly through an inkjet printer. On the market is another is decal-style film (paper-backed) that is printed, peeled and placed down and ironed onto cotton. There is no single method that is superior to the others; they are all different, giving differing effects on cotton to create a hard or soft, shiny or matt surface with clear crisp images or a distressed and faded look.

Heat transfer

This is the simplest and easiest method for quick results and worth trying for many of the paintings or sketches done earlier. It produces soft results that are ready for stitch, but you need to remember that the surface cannot be ironed again, once the image has been transferred onto it.

You will need a reversed digital image from the computer, printed through an inkjet printer onto specialist letterhead-sized (T-shirt) papers.

▶ *On stabilized white cotton, using a very hot dry iron on a firm surface, place the printed image face down and heat press. See the package instructions for timings. Once it begins to cool, peel off the paper.*

▶ *If the image is too shiny, place baking parchment on the surface and lightly iron over it.*

Above: A selection of image-transferred sketches ready for stitch.

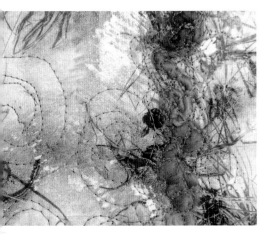

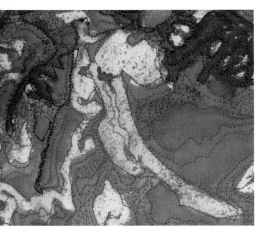

Top and above: Sketchbook collage with
acrylic medium-transfer pages.

Acrylic-medium transfer methods

The various acrylic products will give different effects from clear, colourful, crisp, matt
but plasticized results to some with a good, but duller, image, and others with a more
distressed faded look. Try different media for yourself and decide the style of image
needed for the final stitched piece. A reversed laserjet copy is usually required, but some
results can be achieved from magazine papers, when used with bookbinders' glues.

You will need the following:
• An acrylic medium, such as Picture This (Plaid), Image Maker (Dylon), acrylic gel,
  acrylic matt media or acrylic paint.
• Bookbinders' glues (adhesives) and solvents, which will all work in different ways (pay
  attention to health and safety warnings when using solvents – some might have a
  reaction to certain adhesives).
• A laserjet colour copy in reverse, prepared cotton (prewashed and ironed onto freezer
  paper for stability) and a 5cm (2in) sponge applicator.

Use the applicator to spread the medium thinly onto the surface of the colour copy, and
then lay this face down on the fabric. Ease out any air bubbles and leave it to dry
thoroughly (24 hours or more) in a warm place. Remove the freezer paper and soak the
fabric in water. With an old abrasive sponge, gently rub the backing paper and the image
will appear. After it is dry, a film of paper could appear; this can be removed with a
damp sponge. The transferred image is now ready for sewing (remember that it cannot
be ironed).

Golden (TM) products also work well for image transfer. They are used in a similar
way, but give slightly different, softer results. Bubble Jet Set 2000 is also a popular
method – cotton is soaked in a more dilute liquid acrylic medium, left to dry, stabilized
with freezer paper on cotton, trimmed precisely to letterhead size and printed through
an inkjet printer.

White acrylic paint, matt medium and thinned gesso can also yield results, but the surface
will be more distressed and stiff.

Above: Sketchbook with acrylic-painted pages and image collage. Left: **Outback Sheep Shed** (Sandra Meech, UK). Image transfers on cotton, layered and stitched with Wireform for dimension.

Any combination of the charcoal, oil paint, coloured-pencil and wax-resist techniques covered earlier and worked on paper imagery could be worth trying. There are no 'hard and fast' rules in mixed media – surfaces become expressive and can evolve in a different way than those of more formal paintings. Remember that the mixed-media approach is very appropriate for sketchbooks and board-style books.

Mixed-media exercises

There is a wealth of things to try with mixed media – here are just a few exercises to explore, with fabric and stitch applications included.

Working with black-and-white photocopies

Consider composition when deciding on your subject matter.

▶ *Words and copy, cut or torn from magazines and newspapers, combined with your own writings on a subject, can make a collage composition of squares and rectangles. Use PVA, glue stick or acrylic medium to glue the pieces in place on a firm surface and add acrylic paint or gel medium. On fabric, a similar paper composition (without gel medium) is mounted on thin copier paper in black and white, created for stitch. Add thin interfacing or wadding to the back, and include sheers, organza or stiffened scrim for effect. Machine stitch with a bright colour and have fun with drawing and extending the imagery with the needle.*

▶ *A black-and-white image from a favourite photo is simply coloured with coloured pencil for subtle effects. This has inspired much of my own work over the years.*

▶ *Acrylic paint is applied as a thin wash for one effect and with a palette knife for another, different image.*

Hints
Remember that it is best to use reference material – photographs, writings or printed matter – that you have created yourself, to avoid copyright problems, especially if your work might be published, exhibited or sold. It's worth noting that there are many specialist books available on the numerous methods of photo image transfer that are worth further investigation.

Top and above: Black-and-white and colour-photocopy collage with an acrylic wash. Torn photocopies and painted papers mimic broken ice.

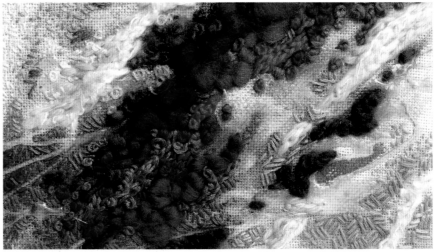

Top left (detail) and right: **Holiday Lets**
(Lynn Creighton, UK). Recycled postcards and
beach-combings. Above: **Kantha Houses**
(detail) (Lynn Creighton, UK). Dyed and vintage
fabrics applied using Kantha stitch.
Right: **Ice Algae** (Sandra Meech, UK). Clear
glue on cotton with wool embroidery using
French knots and seeding stitch.

Colour photocopies from reference

▶ *Create a collaged painting from a photographic source, using a colour copy of the original, magazine pages or your own black-and-white copies, painted with Brusho or watercolour; tear sections to replicate the original. It will never look exactly like the photo, but will have a natural organic and more energetic feel about it. A wash of thin gesso or dilute acrylic could distress the surface. Perhaps this exercise could be taken further with fabric appliqué and the use of sheers?*

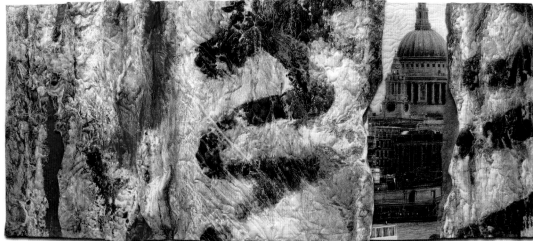

Left and above (detail): **Under the Arches** (Sandra Meech, UK). Graffiti-painted walls, paintings and photographs on cloth layered with wireform and stitched for dimension.

Relief paper exercises

▶ *Low-relief paper combinations suggest a popular exercise to explore dimension and shadow. Taking several small A5 sheets of white or cream paper, use glue to create a number of different textures – scrunched, folded, zigzag, woven, lines, coils, circles and window effects, to name a few. When the glue is completely dry, cut each to at least 7.5cm (3in) square and assemble the pieces together on a firm background. The exercise gives you a chance to imagine how you might work in a similar way with stiffened fabric. Think of as many different combinations as possible and perhaps repeat the exercise, this time with a different composition of cut and shaped samples.*

▶ *Mixed media in low relief – this is another good exercise in white and neutral colours. Collect handmade papers, wallpaper textures, corrugated papers, and combine with anything that has been painted white – hessian, twigs, leaves, sponge, bubble wrap... anything. This could be used as a collagraph print (see page 120).*

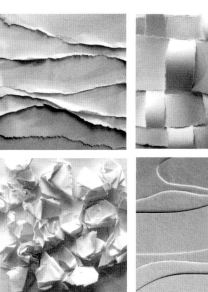

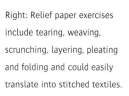
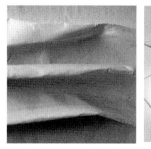

Right: Relief paper exercises include tearing, weaving, scrunching, layering, pleating and folding and could easily translate into stitched textiles.

Art Class 12
Sketch and stitch pages

Perhaps a great place to start with collage is with sketchbook pages, which can become stitchbook pages. Each page can become a collection of writing, drawing, sketching and painting which can easily adapt to fabric and stitch. Composition and design can be explored on a small scale as you consider new themes. Remind yourself of the variety of types of composition that is available to you: remember the rule of thirds (page 20), high and low horizon, block composition, diagonals and curves.

To begin, paint sketchbook pages in the colours of your chosen theme – some will be used for paper collage only and others will be removed for stitching. Consider the following options:
• Brusho-painted black-and-white photocopies that could include handwriting, and colour photocopies of your own images on a personal theme (see page 85).
• Tissue papers, textured wallpapers, type from newspapers or magazines.
• Thinned and evenly spread acrylic paint on cotton will stiffen when dry, but can be torn or cut to page size and used as a background for both paper and fabric.

For stitching, some paper pages will need a thin layer of interfacing to act as a kind of wadding (batting). In other cases, some hand stitches might be explored.

• Any materials could be couched onto the surface – wools, ribbon, net, or small bits of sheer fabric. By now, you will know that anything goes.
• Consider print techniques such as monoprints, screen printing, or stamp effects to create additional interest.
• Remove pages before stitching and consider inserting them into a plastic 2- or 3-ring binder that has been cut down to size. This will allow both sketch and stitch pages to be presented together in the same book.
• Any painted-paper collage could be developed further as a separate composition or stitched with a mix of fabric, scrim and found objects (as illustrated, left). Both collages could be presented on a frame or mounted on a box canvas.

> ### Hint
> Use simple embroidery threads in your machine and a small-holed needle, to keep the paper holes as small as possible. Fancy metallics or twists will be more difficult to work with.

Top left: Mixed-media page from a ringbinder-style sketch and stitch book. Middle and bottom left: **Seaside** (Hilary Beattie, UK). Stitched landscape with papers, fabric and shell detail, and the original paper collage that inspired the piece.

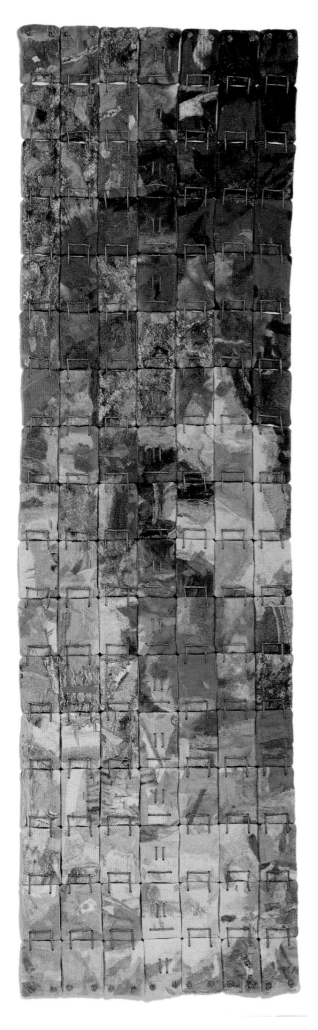

Above and above right (detail): **Soft Stone Armour** (Jackie Smith, UK). This piece was inspired by a set of limestone armour from the Qin dynasty. Constructed fabric from hand-dyed and recycled fabric mixed with hand and machine stitch.

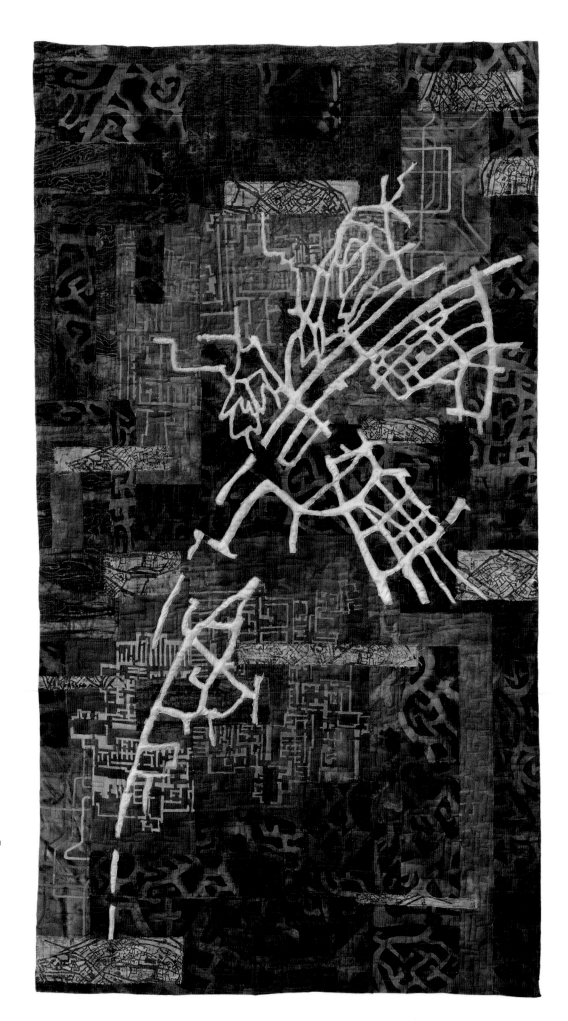

Right: **Delicate Balance**
(Eszter Bornemisza, Hungary)
Layered, printed, dyed and woven
fabrics inspired by old maps.

Art Class 13
Map 'marks'

Study a detailed map, such as a British Ordnance Survey map. Consider the contour lines and marks that indicate historic places, forests, swamps, train lines, rivers, seashore, roads, junctions, boundaries and so on. See how many you can find in a 15cm (6in) square. Create a mixed-media collage that could include transferred photographs, sections of the map, line drawings and painted papers, in a composition backed with thin wadding and stitched through the machine.

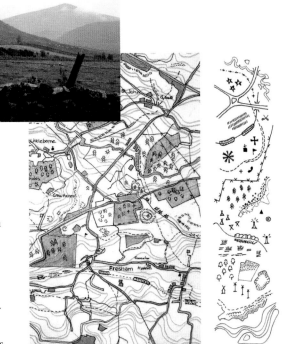

On fabric
- Heat transfer the photo (full or half-page size) from your landscape onto cloth, making sure the image isn't too contrasting in colour and tone. Use the heat-transfer method, adding thin wadding (batting) and backing before you transfer the image.
- Think of another design for stitch. This could be in the form of contour lines, roads and forests. With the original map reference nearby, just go for it on the machine!
- When that is done, hand-stitch marks for any other points of interest.

Art Class 14
Abstract painted collage

This time we are going to create an abstract collage – an emotional response to a theme. This may seem daunting when the 'comfort zone' is realism, but an immediate response in a combination of gels, paints and textures could be more raw and energetic than anything you have ever attempted before. Working with stitch in the same way can be equally liberating. Just go for it and see what happens. Remember that some layers need time to dry before they can be added to.

- Starting with thin canvas or just thick card stock (at least 45 x 60cm/18 x 24in), paint a background colour that will start the mood of the piece, perhaps adding words, magazine or newsprint as you continue to layer with matt medium. Leave this to dry and then perhaps drip some liquid paint on the surface.
- Next, work with any combination of media – photos, words, tissue paper, gesso, texture gels, textured wallpapers and acrylic paint (don't forget the palette knife).
- Continue, perhaps adding a small image or two, then more acrylic and perhaps sgraffitto 'marks'.

There is no right or wrong with this – it is all about expressing yourself and 'letting go'. It may not work perfectly the first time or there may only be a small section of the surface that 'works'. Use the aperture Ls to isolate areas that work well. Photograph them. But remember that allowing yourself the opportunity to have fun is the most important thing.

Top right: Image and map of the Dorset landscape with 'map marks' that can provide inspiration. Right: Painted collage with images and drawings that resembles an old wall.

Mixed-media and print techniques

Mixed media is now frequently incorporated into stitched textiles and this overview of different surface techniques is just an introduction. There is a vast number of books on the market for further exploration and the list on page 127 contains just a small selection.

Collagraphs

A collagraph is a print created from a block of low-relief collage material, such as string, glue patterns, foil, net, hessian, plant materials or just scratched marks. This can then be inked and printed on both paper and fabric or provide a surface for rubbing. Alternatively, it can become an art piece in itself. Jenny Bullen's collagraph print (shown left) shows the intricate detail that can be achieved with a collagraph, which could go on to inspire stitch.

Frottage

Frottage, an extension of collagraphs, is the technique of taking rubbings from a textured surface. This could be from the collagraph plate you have just made or from any wall or floor surface, grid pattern, bits of metal in relief, frosted glass, plastics, or perhaps rubbings from hessian, cheesecloth or bark cloth – in fact, any textured material, natural or manmade. Rub the surface with oil pastels, water-soluble pastels or soft coloured pencils to create interesting surfaces.

Laminating

Laminating is an extension of collage, in which thin sheets of tissue paper are glued together with dilute PVA glue (white craft glue) to create layers of translucent colour. Rubbings with oil pastels, Markal Paintstiks or soft coloured pencil can be added for interesting effects. This could inspire stitch marks on sheer fabrics bonded with fusible webbing.

In addition to paper only, printed images, written scraps of text or drawings could be trapped and glued between layers of tissue paper. Taking this further with sheers and stitch, you could use fusible webbing such as Bondaweb (Wonder Under), Mistyfuse, Stitch Witchery or light adhesive glues to bond the fabric. Printed images could be transferred directly onto sheers or transferred onto cotton and trapped, perhaps adding snips of threads or other 'bits' for interest.

It is also possible to add several layers of fusible webbing ironed onto the coloured side of an inkjet printout (use 'parchment' paper). The white paper back is soaked and removed to leave a surface which can be layered onto fabric and stitched.

Left: **Collagraph Inspiration** (Jenny Bullen, UK).
Exciting images on paper or fabric.
Opposite page, top and bottom: Landscape with monoprinted and transfer-dyed fabric with paper and stitch.

Monoprinting

Monoprinting is another simple way to make a single print with marks that are very different to those that are painted or drawn. The surface can be anything that is smooth, flat and non-absorbent, such as plastic sheet, glass or glossy thick card. Apply oil paint or printing inks with a variety of tools, such as brushes, rollers, sticks, sponges or palette knives, as you build the design. A piece of paper is laid over the surface while wet and it is then rubbed or rolled firmly. When lifted, the print is in reverse on the paper.

Prints on acetate or glass offer a different style of monoprint.

▶ *Screen-printing inks are rolled thinly onto the smooth surface; working quickly, marks or pattern or lines are drawn into it with the end of a brush, palette knife or scraping tool. Lay paper on immediately; press firmly with a large clean roller, and pull off a print. This can be also done on stabilized cotton.*

▶ *Alternatively, ink the surface as before; lay the paper or cloth down immediately, and draw from the back. This might be interesting if different colours of ink are laid down initially.*

Linocuts

These need to be mentioned as they can also provide wonderful printed impressions, both on paper and cloth, and are great for a beginner to printmaking. Original images are created on the surface of the linoleum with gouging and v-tools. Draw a simple illustration or pattern on the surface first. Roll printing ink evenly; lay paper on top, and rub with the back of a spoon, pressing it over the surface (a printing press may give more even and darker results). This is very appropriate for cloth and can create wonderful graphic imagery in stitched textiles.

Screen printing

This is another very popular print technique to consider for surface cloth techniques. It is not a print from a direct impression (one surface to another), but is made through an intermediate material – a screen mesh. Prepared screens, squeegees and screen-printing inks for this purpose are available at most art shops. Clean or crisp images on the screen can be created with a hand-cut film stencil that becomes part of the screen or from torn and cut paper shapes, placed underneath.

Recently, Thermofax screen-printing techniques have become more readily available, enabling many textile artists with their own digital imagery to order screens online. As they are usually mounted on card, they have become a relatively inexpensive option. At one time, screen printing on fabric was rare in art quilts; now it is frequently used. There are many good classes and books available for those who wish to explore this in greater depth. When combined with good composition and other collaged materials, screen printing can be extremely effective.

Hints

- Stabilize cotton with freezer paper for a firmer surface for any print or surface techniques.
- Don't forget that any interesting prints on paper could be heat transferred onto cloth for stitch.
- Always have water and cleaning equipment nearby as acrylic screen inks dry quickly.

Art Class 15
Walls that speak

- Every textile artist has at some time been fascinated with old walls – walls with paint peeling, cracks, damp or rust marks or more recent walls, decorated with graffiti. Collect as many images you have (or take some new photos) and consider how you could replicate these on a small stretched canvas with gesso, built-up textures and acrylic paint. Perhaps there is a message or two on the wall?
- Torn posters hold the same kind of interest, including mixed messages, words and statements that overlap and blend. We all try and read what they say. This is an opportunity to re-create a poster wall on a prepared canvas, covered with layers of paper, gesso and more paper, peeled back several times.
- A photograph of a torn poster wall has also been photo transferred onto cotton and cut through to mimic the kind of paper dimension you might see on a real wall.

Left: **Posterwall, Limerick** (Sandra Meech, UK).

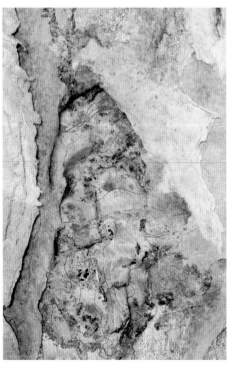

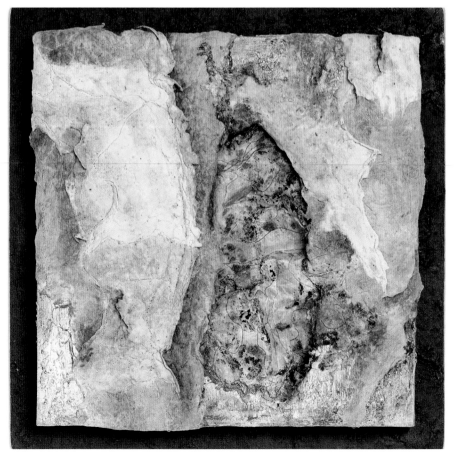

Above (detail) and right: **Parete 1** (Jacky Russell, UK).
Crumbling walls in Venice.

Above and left (detail): **Iron Lace** (Linda Colsh, Belgium/USA). Dramatic but subtle imagery.

Above: Mixed-media collage mounted 'off the wall' for added dimension.

Presenting art textiles

Working with fine art disciplines has perhaps made you consider the way you will want work presented in the future. For exhibitions with white walls and good lighting, perhaps it is time to think like a gallery artist.

▶ *Art quilts can be dramatic without a frame, providing they hang flat and straight. Weighting a quilt with an additional baton in a bottom sleeve is one answer. Keep quilts rolled (with the good side out) rather than folded. Smaller contemporary quilts can be mounted onto a canvas box frame and either sewn or attached with Velcro. Perhaps you might stretch a quilted piece over foam board, which gives a painterly feel to your textile art.*

▶ *Stitched textiles and embroidered pieces could also be presented on a box canvas frame. If framing in a conventional way, keep it modern and simple so it doesn't detract from the work. Textiles can be mounted directly onto the cardboard backing panel or perhaps stretched over foamboard first. Use a deeper box-style frame if glass is to be used, so the textile isn't pressed tightly. Unless the glass is free of glare, it will detract from the finished piece; on the other hand, customers like to see work displayed behind glass.*

▶ *Dimensional work, if small, could be set in a very deep box frame. This presentation can create a certain mood for the stitched textile as well as protecting it.*

Above: A collagraph can be painted and mounted as a mixed-media installation.
Right: **Pentimento 22** (Jette Clover, Belgium).

CONCLUSION

By now your head may be spinning with new ideas and creative approaches to explore. It is like a circle that goes round and round, back to the roots of art and drawing and the line that becomes the stitched mark. That constant connection between art and stitch is what it is all about and what makes our life in stitched textiles so exciting.

An art and graphic design background has given me a different starting point to that of most people involved in stitched textiles. Early training helped me to see the world through an artist's eyes, but 15 years ago I chose to work with different media – fabric and stitch. Photography is important to my work, but it's not just about taking pictures. I still love the challenge of drawing and painting, but would miss the texture and dimension offered by stitched textiles. Mixing art and stitched textiles together has given me the greatest satisfaction and the most exciting challenge so far. I hope that after reading this book, you feel the same.

Above: **Up Sticks** (Sandra Meech, UK). Trees that are being cut down and forests that are in decline because of global warming or urban development have long been subjects close to my heart.

ART GLOSSARY

Abstract Art that is based on colour and form rather than realism.
Abstract Expressionism A style of painting based on the expression of the subconscious.
Acrylic A quick-drying permanent and colourfast paint, consisting of pigment suspended in a synthetic medium, that is relatively new in the art world.

Binder A liquid medium that is mixed with pigment to form paint or oil-pastel sticks. Different types of binder are used for different media: gum arabic for watercolour, oil for oil paints, and a synthetic resin for acrylics.
Blending In painting, the gradual transition from a light to a dark colour or merging one colour to another so the joins are not visible. Coloured pencils need to be soft to blend well.
Blocking in Areas of colour and tone added at the beginning of a painting to establish its basic composition.

Calligraphy The art of decorative writing. Calligraphy pens make wonderful irregular, energetic marks as the lines they make can be both thick and thin.
Canvas The heavy woven fabric used to support an acrylic or oil painting. In textiles canvas is often used with texture mediums or gesso with big stitch.
Cartoon A quick drawing or sketch, sometimes in the form of a comic caricature.
Collage The technique of forming a picture or surface design by pasting on a mix of materials that could include paper, photographs, newspaper cuttings, fabrics and sometimes stitch on a flat surface. Texture gels can be also used.
Colour The **primary colours** are red, blue and yellow in painting and magenta, cyan and yellow in printing. These pigments cannot be obtained from other colours. **Secondary colours** are the primaries mixed to form green, purple and orange, and **tertiary colours** are ones mixed from adjacent primary and secondary colours (for example, green and blue make turquoise). **Complementary colours** lie opposite each other on the colour wheel. These pairs of colours – red and green, yellow and purple, and blue and orange – are widely seen in nature, and when seen together are dynamic and energetic. A **monochrome** painting is one that uses only one colour or hue mixed with black and white to create different tones. **Analogous colours** are at least three adjacent colours on the colour wheel

that form a harmonious arrangement. A dynamic combination would include analogous colours with a touch of the colour opposite on the wheel (for example, yellow, orange and red with a small amount of cold blue).
Composition The arrangement and combination of elements in a painting or surface. The triangular composition is often seen in still-life arrangements.
Crosshatching A mark-making technique used for building up shadow, consisting of layers of crisscrossed lines instead of a solid tone.
Cubism The art style developed by Picasso and Braque around 1908, which breaks down natural forms into geometric shapes. In cubism, perspective is not fixed and often a subject is viewed from many sides.

Expressionism An art movement of the early 1900s in which realism and proportion was replaced by an emotional connection to the subject. Often paintings were abstract, with the subject and colour distorted.

Figurative painting Painting that takes a real rather than an abstract subject (which doesn't always have to include the human form).

Glazing The application of oil or acrylic colour in thin, transparent layers so the base colour shows through. Watercolour washes are overlaid on each other and although they are transparent, are still called glazes, which can be misleading.
Gouache Opaque watercolour paint, similar to poster paint, which is often used in illustration.

Hatching A technique that uses parallel lines to indicate form, shadow and tone.
Horizon line The imaginary line at eye level when viewing a subject or landscape and where the vanishing point or points are located. In perspective, the horizon line should not be confused with the line where the land and sky meet, which could be higher or lower than one's eye level.

Impasto Paint applied thickly to a surface to create texture.
Impressionism A style of painting of the late 19th century that used broken colour for an atmospheric, visual impression of the subject. In Impressionist paintings, light is depicted in short brushstrokes that appear broken on the surface but, when seen from a distance, became recombined in the viewer's eye. This effect is known as optical mixture.

Lifting out A technique used to remove wet paint, usually watercolour or gouache, from the surface of a painting with a brush, sponge or tissue. This will soften the edges, reduce the intensity of the colour or create a subtle highlight. This is often used in cloud effects.

Mixed media A popular technique using two or more types of media. For the textile artist these could include art media – watercolour, gouache, acrylic paint – plus paper, fabric and stitch.

Negative space The space around an object rather than the shape itself.

Perspective The way of representing a subject to give the impression of depth on a flat surface.
Linear perspective is used when receding parallel lines seem to converge at a point on the horizon.
Pointillism The technique of applying colour in dots rather than lines or strokes on the surface. This could easily adapt to the use of French knots in embroidery for the same effect.

Realism The artistic style that takes inspiration from everyday life.
Resists Masking fluid is a latex liquid which is applied by brush to mask out areas of an artwork. After paint is applied fluid can be rubbed away. Other resists like white candle wax, oil pastel or wax on cloth will mask areas to resist paint or dye for interesting effects.
Rule of thirds Based on the Golden Section, the rule of thirds is the system of organizing proportions of a composition to create a centre of interest and harmonious effect over a surface. When the area is broken into thirds, vertically and horizontally, the point where two lines meet becomes a focal point, balanced by the point in the opposite corner. It allows for the eye to move around the surface of the painting more easily.

Sgraffito The technique of scratching into a coloured surface to create texture, using a sharp instrument such as a knife or a pin.

Tone or value is the lightness or darkness of any areas of the subject regardless of colour. Tone in colour terms relates to some colour hues that are naturally lighter than others, for example yellow compared with purple.

Wash The application of dilute colour spread transparently (thinly) over the surface of a painting.

BIBLIOGRAPHY

Atkinson, Jennifer, Holly Harrison and Paula Grasdal. *Collage Sourcebook: Exploring the Art and Techniques of Collage.* Apple Press, 2004

Beam, Mary Todd. *Celebrate Your Creative Self.* North Light, 2001

Brommer, Gerald. *Collage Techniques: A Guide for Artists and Illustrators.* Watson-Guptill, 1994

Cartwright, Angel. *Mixed Emulsions: Altered Art Techniques for Photographic Imagery.* Rockport Publishers, 2007

Desmet, Anne and Jim Anderson. *Handmade Prints: An Introduction to Creative Printmaking Without a Press.* A & C Black, 2005

Diehn, Gwen. *The Decorated Page.* Lark Books, 2003

Dunnewold, Jane. *Complex Cloth.* Fibre Studio Press, 1996.

Genders, Carolyn. *Sources of Inspiration.* A & C Black, 2008

Green, Jean Drysdale. *Arteffects.* Watson Guptill, 1993

Greenlees, Kay. *Creating Sketchbooks for Embroiderers and Textile Artists.* Batsford, 2005

Grey, Maggie. *Raising the Surface with Machine Embroidery.* Batsford, 2004

Grey, Maggie and Jane Wild. *Paper, Metal and Stitch.* Batsford, 2005

Hartill, Brenda and Richard Clarke. *Collagraphs and Mixed-Media Printmaking.* A & C Black Publishers, 2008

La Plantz, Shereen. *Cover to Cover.* Lark Books, 1998.

Laury, Jean Ray. *Imagery on Fabric.* C & T Publishing, 1997

Leland, Nita. *The Creative Artist.* North Light, 2006

New, Jennifer. *Drawing from Life: The Journal as Art.* Princeton Architectural Press, 2005

Oei, Loan and Cecile de Kegel. *The Elements of Design.* Thames & Hudson, 2002

Perrella, Lynne. *Artists' Journals and Sketchbooks: Exploring and Creating Personal Pages.* Quarry Books, 2004

Perry, Vicky. *Abstract Painting: Concepts and Techniques.* Watson-Guptill, 2005

Peterson, Bryan. *Learning to See Creatively: Design, Color and Composition in Photography.* Amphoto Books, 2003

Reiter, Laura. *Learn to Paint Abstracts.* Collins, 2006

Roberts, Ian. *Mastering Composition: Techniques and Principles to Dramatically Improve Your Painting.* North Light, 2007

Scott, Marilyn. *The Acrylic Artist's Bible.* Search Press, 2005

Simpson, Ian. *Drawing, Seeing and Observation.* A & C Black, 2009

Springall, Diana. *Inspired to Stitch: 21 Textile Artists.* A & C Black, 2008

Stobart, Jane. *Drawing Matters.* A & C Black, 2008

Tauchid, Rheni. *The New Acrylics: A Complete Guide to the New Generation of Acrylic Paints.* Watson-Guptill, 2005

van Vliet, Rolina. *Painting Abstracts: Ideas, Projects and Techniques.* Search Press, 2008

SUPPLIERS

UK
Bovilles Art Shops
Tel: 01895 450300
www.bovilles.co.uk

Seawhite of Brighton
Tel: 01403 711633
www.seawhite.co.uk

Art Van Go
Tel: 01438 814946
www.artvango.co.uk

Rainbow Silks
Tel: 01494 862111
www.rainbowsilks.co.uk

Colourcraft
Tel: 0114 242 1431
www.colourcraftltd.com

Kemtex Colours
Tel: 01257 230220
www.kemtex.co.uk

Freudenberg Nonwovens
(Vilene interfacings)
Tel: 01422 327900
www.nonwovens-group.com

Whaleys (Bradford) Ltd
Tel: 01274 521309
www.whaleys-bradford.ltd.uk

USA
Dick Blick Art Materials
Tel: 1-800-828-4548
www.dickblick.com

Dharma Trading Company
www.dharmatrading.com
Tel: 1-800-542-5227

PRO Chemical & Dye, Inc
Tel: 1-800-228-9393
www.prochemical.com

Canada
Currys Art supplies
Tel: 1-800-268-2969
www.currys.com

G&S Dyes & Accessories Ltd
Tel: 1-800-596-0550
www.gsdye.com

Groups
Quilt Art
www.quiltart.org.uk

The Quilters' Guild of the British Isles
www.quiltersguild.org.uk

Canadian Quilters' Association
www.canadianquilter.com

Embroiderers' Guild
www.embroderersguild.com

Sandra Meech
www.sandrameech.com

INDEX

abstract art 13
abstract expressionism 34
abstract from photo reference 99
abstract, a step into 34
acrylics 92–96
altered books 87
aperture Ls 42
appliqué 9
Art Class 1: Layer, scrunch, fold and draw 43
Art Class 2: Tonal collage 45
Art class 3: Building detail in line and tone 51
Art Class 4: Still life in black and white 53
Art Class 5: Art as inspiration 58
Art Class 6: Moving marks 60
Art Class 7: Wet media still life 84
Art Class 8: Reflections and stitch 91
Art Class 9: Into the abstract 99
Art Class 10: Getting in the mood 103
Art Class 11: Working in series 104
Art Class 12: Sketch and stitch pages 116
Art Class 13: Map 'marks' 119
Art Class 14: Abstract painted collage 119
Art Class 15: Walls that speak 122
art materials 16
art textiles, presenting 124
Ash, Bethan 50

Barton, Elizabeth 25, 51
Beattie, Hilary 116
Benner, Sue 35, 62
bibliography 127
black-and-white photocopies 113
bleach pen 53
boards 38
Bornemisza, Eszter 118
Brimelow, Elizabeth 18, 19
Brusho 85
buildings 13, 25

Caldwell, Dorothy 7, 47
calligraphy pen 38, 84
charcoal 44
chinagraph marker 38, 75
ChromaCoal 44, 48

cityscapes 24
clingfilm (Saran Wrap) 75
Clover, Jette 13, 124
collage 11, 108–110
collagraph 120, 124
collectibles and hobbies 31
colour 63–65
Colsh, Linda 123
composition, still-life 26
conté techniques 44
Creighton, Lynn 63, 114
Curtis, Bailey 20, 21

disperse transfer dyes 76–79
Dove, Sue 36
drawing animals 29
drawing from life 29
drawing in line 49
drawing materials, cloth 38, 39
drawing-pen techniques 46
drawing people 29
drawing portraits 29
drawing, quick sketches 41

Edwards, Mair 109
elements, placing of 26
erasers 38, 44

freezer paper 39
frottage 120

gel mediums 109
Ginsberg, Mandy 106
Gleave, Linda 68
glossary 126
gouache 82, 91

Hueber, Inge 12

Impey, Sara 32
impressing 42, 75
Impressionist movement 34
Ingres paper 48
inkjet transfer paper 39

journals 87

laminating 120
landscape 12, 23, 53
left-brain drawing 60
line and tone 41
linocuts 121
Lutradur 110, 111
Maries, Jae 28, 101

Markal Paintstiks 57
marker techniques 46
mark-making 37, 44
Martin, Cherilyn, 61
masking fluid 75
media 33
memorabilia 31
Michael, Kris 31
mixed media 11, 13, 107, 113, 120
monoprinting 121

Nash, Dominie 10, 27
nature subjects 22
negative composition 48
newspapers and magazines 33
Newton, Amelia 109

oil paints 101
oil pastel on cotton 58
oil pastel effects 56
oil pastels 109
oil paint techniques 101
oil paints on fabric 102

painting 9, 69
painting materials 70
painting techniques 69
Paintshop Pro 14
paper 38
pastels 38, 57, 84
pencil exercises 41
pencils, coloured 54, 55
pencils, graphite 38
perle cotton 40
perspective 20
photo filters 24
photo image transfer 11, 94, 111
photo transfer, acrylic medium 112
photo transfer, heat 111

photographs, using 11, 16
photography 14–16
photos, transferred 31
Photoshop Elements 14, 25, 66, 69, 102
Photoshop filters 49
piecing 9
plastics, bonded 111
pointillism 48, 49
politics 33
polyester sateen 49, 79
portrait and figure drawing 13
positive and negative shapes 26, 31
posters and graffiti 24, 32

reflections 13
relief paper exercises 115
resists 38 75
rule of thirds 21
Russell, Jacky 122

scaling up/enlarging 22
Schwartz Smith, Lura 15, 30, 99
screen printing 121
sgraffito 53
sketchbooks 20, 38, 87, 88
Smith, Barbara Lee 110
Smith, Jackie 117
social comment 33
soluble materials 9, 57
spontaneity 58
staywet palette 71
still life 12, 26
still-life tonal composition 45
still-life watercolour 76
stitch skills, drawing 9, 40
studio space 8
subjects and design 19
suppliers 127
surface techniques 11
Surgenor, Freda 24, 26, 77, 27, 7

textures 9, 40
thermofax 121
Thomson, Tom 58
tints and shades 65
tonal values 15
tone and tonal sketching 22
tracing paper, graphite 45
transparency 9
Twinn, Janet 67

Van Baarle, Els 33
Van der Hoorst Beetsma, Dirkje 52
Vold Klausen, Bente 33, 34

wadding (batting) 40
Wagner, Esther 99
watercolour 72–76
wax crayons 57
wet-on-wet watercolour 72, 76
window templates 20
wools 40
words of inspiration 58

Yde, Charlotte 49, 104, 105